教科書ガイド

三省堂 版

マイウェイ
English
Communication Ⅲ

TEXT

BOOK

GUIDE

JN062980

文研出版

はじめに

　本書は、三省堂発行の高等学校の英語教科書『MY WAY English Communication III』で学習するみなさんの予習と演習のために執筆されました。

　英語の勉強は事前に自ら調べ、また、授業のあとで復習し演習することで、学習した内容を確かなものにすることができます。本書はこうした予習と演習をより効果的に進めることを目的に作られた案内書であり、教科書本文の日本語訳や問題の解答をそのまま与えるものではありません。

　本書では、教科書の内容を正しく理解するだけでなく、教科書で扱われる表現や文法の体系をわかりやすく解説し、さらに多くの例題を解くことによりその定着をはかることを目指しました。本書を教科書本文の理解に役立たせるばかりでなく、みなさんが積極的に英語でコミュニケーションを行う手がかりとして利用していただければ幸いです。

2024年2月

編集部

本書の構成と使用上の注意

● 教科書本文と A B C 単語・語句の研究

　　レッスンの本文をセクションごとに転載し、「読解のポイント」を提示しています。また、そのセクションの新出語句をチェック欄とともに本文の下に掲載しています。例や参考も語彙を広げるのに役立ちます。

● 解説

　　本文を理解する上で重要な箇所を取り上げ、文型、文法、および語句や表現の観点からわかりやすく解説してあります。解説のあとの ✐確認 では、解説の要点を理解できているかどうかを確認することができます。

● 確認問題

　　UNIT 2・3では各レッスンの最後に確認問題を入れています。段階を踏んで英語の理解を総合的に確認できるように、次のような内容で3～4ページ構成になっています。

前半の大問（語彙・表現・文法問題）：

　　教科書で学んだ語彙・表現・文型・文法・語法などについて、演習します。

後半の大問（総合問題）：

　　教科書本文の抜粋を掲載し、英文和訳・和文英訳・整序問題などを設けました。内容・要点の把握と理解を総合的に確認します。

CONTENTS

UNIT 1

UNIT 2

UNIT 3

UNIT 1

Reading Skill 1-8

Blended Words

 読解のポイント 教科書 p.14

1. 混成語とは何ですか。
2. 混成語の具体例として、どのような語がありますか。

Setting **You are reading a blog about new English words.**

There are many blended words in English. ① You may be using them without knowing it. ② A blended word is created by combining two different words.

Let's look at some examples. ③ What would you call a meal that you have at around 11:00 a.m.? It's too late for breakfast and too early for lunch. ④ Yes, you call it "brunch." "Brunch" is a blend of breakfast and lunch. "Brexit" is a more recent example. ⑤ The word concisely explains that Great Britain exited from the EU.

⑥ Lastly, can you guess the meaning of the word "snaccident"? ⑦ Let's say you have a snack, such as a pack of cookies, and decide to eat just one cookie. ⑧ However, you can't stop eating and finish the whole pack by accident. ⑨ That's a "snaccident"! ⑩ Blended words show how flexibly people use English.

単語・語句の研究

☐ **blend (ed)** [blénd(id)]	動 ～を混合する
☐ blended words	混成語
☐ **combining** [kəmbáiniŋ] ＜ **combine**	動 ～を結合させる、～を組み合わせる
☐ **brunch** [bríntʃ]	名 ブランチ、朝昼兼用の食事 参考 breakfast（朝食）、lunch（昼食）
☐ **Brexit** [brégzit]	名 ブレグジット、英国のEU離脱 参考 Britain（英国）、exit（退去、退出）
☐ **recent** [ríːsnt]	形 最近の、新しい 参考 recently（最近）

□ concisely [kənsáisli]　　　　　副 簡潔に　**参考** concise（簡潔な）

□ Great Britain [grèit brítn]　　　名 英国、イギリス

□ snaccident [snǽksədənt]　　　名 スナックシデント（お菓子などをつい完食してしまうこと）
参考 snack（軽食、スナック）、accident（事故、不測の出来事）

□ flexibly [fléksəbli]　　　　　副 柔軟に　**参考** flexible（柔軟な）

 解説

① **You may be using them without knowing it.**
- 助動詞 may のあとに進行形〈be 動詞＋動詞の ing 形〉が続いている文。「〜しているかもしれない」の意味。助動詞のあとには動詞の原形がくるので、be 動詞は原形の be になっている。
- **確認** （　）内に適切な語を入れなさい。
　ア．私の父はキッチンで夕食を作っているかもしれない。
　　　My father (　　　) (　　　) cooking dinner in the kitchen.
　イ．彼らは川で泳いでいるかもしれない。
　　　They (　　　) be (　　　) in the river.
- them は前文の blended words をさす。

② **A blended word is created by combining two different words.**
- 〈be 動詞＋過去分詞〉「〜され（てい）る」という受け身の文。
- combining は動名詞。by 〜ing は「〜することによって」の意味で、手段や方法を表している。

③ **What would you call a meal that you have at around 11:00 a.m.?**
- that は関係代名詞で、that 以下が先行詞 a meal を後ろから修飾している。
- meal は「食事」の意味。

④ **Yes, you call it "brunch."**
- 〈call ＋ O ＋ C〉で「O を C と呼ぶ」の意味。ここでは、O = it、C = "brunch" である。
- it は③の a meal that you have at around 11:00 a.m. をさす。

⑤ **The word concisely explains that Great Britain exited from the EU.**
- The word は前文の "Brexit" をさす。
- that は接続詞。explain that ～は「～ということを説明する」の意味。
- exit は「出ていく」の意味。
- the EU は the European Union の略で、「欧州連合、ヨーロッパ連合」のこと。2020年に英国は EU を離脱した。

⑥ **Lastly, can you guess the meaning of the word "snaccident"?**
- lastly は「最後に」、guess は「～を推測する」、meaning は「意味」の意味。

⑦ **Let's say you have a snack, such as a pack of cookies, and decide to eat just one cookie.**
- let's say は「例えば」の意味。
- such as a pack of cookies「例えばクッキー1箱」は a snack の例として挙げられている。
- decide to ～は「～することにする」の意味。
- just one cookie は「クッキーを1枚だけ」ということ。

⑧ **However, you can't stop eating and finish the whole pack by accident.**
- stop ～ing は「～するのをやめる」、whole は「すべての、まるまる」、by accident は「たまたま、誤って」の意味。

⑨ **That's a "snaccident"!**
- That は⑦・⑧全体の内容をさす。

⑩ **Blended words show how flexibly people use English.**
- how flexibly people use English は「人々がどれほど柔軟に英語を使うか」という意味の間接疑問文。〈how + 副詞 + S + V〉で「S がどれほど…に～するか」という意味。
- **確認** (　　) 内に適切な語を入れなさい。
  - ア．私はリカオンがどれほど効率的に狩りをするか知っている。
    I know (　　) efficiently African hunting dogs hunt.
  - イ．彼女はその機械がどれほど精密に作られているかに気づいた。
    She noticed (　　) precisely the machine was made.

READING SKILL 2

London — National Park City

 読解のポイント

教科書 p.18

1. ロンドンはどのような都市を目指していますか。
2. 自然保護はどのようなことにつながるでしょうか。

Setting You are reading a newspaper article about London.

① When you hear of London, you may think of Big Ben, a double-decker bus, or fish and chips. Actually, London is also famous as a green city. ② It has about 3,000 parks and almost as many trees as its population. ③ Nearly 15,000 species of animals and plants live in the city.

④ In 2019, London declared that it would become the world's first National Park City. ⑤ With this declaration, London aims to keep its green areas and turn itself into a healthier city. One reason for this is the expected population growth. ⑥ It is possible that the green areas will be destroyed for building houses.

⑦ The starting point of this declaration was a proposal by a high school geography teacher. ⑧ He believed that preserving nature in the city would be a countermeasure against climate change. ⑨ He also thought that it would provide playgrounds for children and habitats for wildlife.

Now several cities in the UK, the US, and Australia are following this trend. ⑩ This movement may spread further across the world.

🄰🄱🄲 単語・語句の研究

☐ Big Ben [bíg bén]	名 ビッグベン ((英国国会議事堂時計塔))
☐ double-decker [dʌbldékər]	形 二階建ての
☐ chip (s) [tʃíp(s)]	名 フライドポテト (イギリス英語)
☐ as many 〜 as ...	…と同じくらい多くの〜 例 I have as many sneakers as you. (私はあなたと同じくらい多くのスニーカーを持っている)
☐ population [pɑ̀pjəléiʃn]	名 人口

☐ **declare (d)** [dikléər(d)]	動 ～を宣言する
☐ **declaration** [dèkləréiʃn]	名 宣言、声明
☐ turn ～ into ...	～を…に変える
☐ **growth** [gróuθ]	名 増加、成長 参考 grow（増える、成長する）
☐ **proposal** [prəpóuzl]	名 提案　参考 propose（～を提案する）
☐ countermeasure [káuntərmèʒər]	名 対策 参考 counter（反対の）、measure（手段）
☐ **climate** [kláimət]	名 気候

解説

① **When you hear of London, you may think of Big Ben, a double-decker bus, or fish and chips.**
- hear of ～は「～のことを耳にする」、think of ～は「～を思い出す、考えつく」の意味。
- fish and chips「フィッシュアンドチップス」は、魚（タラなど）のフライとフライドポテトの盛り合わせのこと。英国の大衆的な料理。

② **It has about 3,000 parks and almost as many trees as its population.**
- Itは前文のLondonをさす。
- its populationはロンドンの人口をさす。ロンドンの人口は約900万人。

③ **Nearly 15,000 species of animals and plants live in the city.**
- Nearly ～plantsがこの文の主語。
- nearlyは「ほぼ、ほとんど」、speciesは「（生物の）種」、plantは「植物」の意味。
- the cityはロンドンをさす。

④ **In 2019, London declared that it would become the world's first National Park City.**
- thatは接続詞で、declare that ～は「～ということを宣言する」の意味。
- that節内のitはLondonをさす。
- 過去の文なので、that節内の（助）動詞も時制の一致で過去形になるため、willではなくwouldが使われている。
- National Park Cityは「国立公園都市」の意味。

⑤ **With this declaration, London aims to keep its green areas and turn itself into a healthier city.**
- aim to ～は「～することを目指す」、green area は「緑地」の意味。
- its、itself は London をさす。
- healthy は「健康な、健康によい」の意味で、ここでは比較級になっている。

⑥ **It is possible that the green areas will be destroyed for building houses.**
- It is possible that ... は「…ということが起こりうる」の意味。
- that 節内は助動詞 will を使った受け身の文。〈will be ＋過去分詞〉で「～されるだろう」の意味。
- destroy は「～を破壊する」の意味。

⑦ **The starting point of this declaration was a proposal by a high school geography teacher.**
- starting point は「出発点、原点」、geography は「地理」の意味。

⑧ **He believed that preserving nature in the city would be a countermeasure against climate change.**
- that は接続詞。believe that ～で「～ということを信じる」の意味。
- preserving nature in the city が that 節内の主語。preserve は「～を保存する、守る」の意味で、ここでは動名詞になっている。
- 過去の文なので、時制の一致で that 節内の助動詞も過去形（would）になっている。
- climate change は「気候変動」の意味。

⑨ **He also thought that it would provide playgrounds for children and habitats for wildlife.**
- that は接続詞。think that ～で「～ということを考える、思う」の意味。
- that 節内の主語 it は⑧の preserving nature in the city をさす。
- provide ～ for ... は「…に～を与える、提供する」、playground は「遊び場」、habitat は「（動植物の）生息地、すみか」、wildlife は「野生生物」の意味。

⑩ **This movement may spread further across the world.**
- movement は「（社会的）運動」、spread は「広がる」、further は「さらに遠くへ」、across the world は「世界中に［で］」の意味。

Flying Cars

 読解のポイント

教科書 p.22

1. スロバキアの空飛ぶ車はどのようなものですか。
2. 空飛ぶ車にはどのような問題が残っていますか。

Setting **You are reading a magazine article on science.**

① Many people experience heavy traffic jams every day. ② They must be worried about being late for school or work. ③ What if cars could take off suddenly from the road and fly to their destinations? ④ In fact, flying cars are not just science fiction any longer.

⑤ In 2021, a car actually flew in an experiment conducted in Slovakia. ⑥ It has retractable wings and a propeller in its rear. ⑦ The car successfully flew between two cities and drove safely after landing. ⑧ A Japanese start-up also began marketing a flying car, which has many propellers for taking off vertically. ⑨ Likewise, an American company introduced the image of an electric flying car with four large propellers for moving like a drone.

⑩ Although there remain several issues such as setting safety standards, it will not be long before people can drive a flying car.

A B C 単語・語句の研究

☐ what if 〜?	〜したらどうなるだろうか。 例 What if he can't come to the game? (彼が試合に来られなかったらどうなるだろうか)
☐ take off	(飛行機などが) 離陸する 例 The plane will take off in 30 minutes. (その飛行機は30分後に離陸する)
☐ **destination (s)** [dèstənéiʃn(z)]	名 目的地、行き先
☐ not 〜 any longer	もはや〜でない 例 The documents don't exist any longer. (その文書はもはや存在しない)
☐ **fiction** [fíkʃn]	名 小説、フィクション

☐ **conduct (ed)** [kəndʌ́kt(id)]	動 ～を行う	
☐ Slovakia [slouvɑ́:kiə]	名 スロバキア((ヨーロッパ中部の国))	
☐ retractable [ritrǽktəbl]	形 格納式の	
☐ propeller [prəpélər]	名 プロペラ	
☐ **rear** [ríər]	名 後部、後方	
☐ start-up [stɑ́:rtʌ̀p]	名 新設企業、設立したばかりの会社	
☐ vertically [vɘ́:rtikli]	副 垂直に **参考** vertical（垂直の）	
☐ **electric** [iléktrik]	形 電気の、電動の **参考** electricity（電気）	
☐ drone [dróun]	名 ドローン	
☐ it will not be long before ～	まもなく～だろう	

例 It will not be long before space travel becomes common.
（まもなく宇宙旅行が一般的になるだろう）

 解説

① **Many people experience heavy traffic jams every day.**
- experienceは「～を経験する」、traffic jamは「交通渋滞」の意味。

② **They must be worried about being late for school or work.**
- mustは「～に違いない」、be worried about ～は「～を心配している」の意味。

③ **What if cars could take off suddenly from the road and fly to their destinations?**
- 仮定法の文なので、過去の助動詞couldが使われている。
- suddenlyは「突然、急に」の意味。

④ **In fact, flying cars are not just science fiction any longer.**
- in factは「実際は」、science fictionは「空想科学小説、SF」の意味。
- flyingは動名詞で、flying carsがこの文の主語。

⑤ **In 2021, a car actually flew in an experiment conducted in Slovakia.**
- actuallyは「実際に、本当に」、experimentは「実験」の意味。
- flewはfly「飛ぶ」の過去形。

- conducted は過去分詞で、conducted in Slovakia が an experiment を後ろから修飾している。

⑥ **It has retractable wings and a propeller in its rear.**
  - It は⑤の a car をさす。
  - wing は「翼」の意味。

⑦ **The car successfully flew between two cities and drove safely after landing.**
  - successfully は「うまく、成功のうちに」、safely は「安全に」、landing は「着陸」の意味。
  - drove は drive「運転される」の過去形。

⑧ **A Japanese start-up also began marketing a flying car, which has many propellers for taking off vertically.**
  - begin ～ing は「～し始める」、market は「～を市場に出す」の意味。
  - which は関係代名詞 (非制限用法) で、「そしてそれは～」と先行詞 a flying car を説明している。

⑨ **Likewise, an American company introduced the image of an electric flying car with four large propellers for moving like a drone.**
  - likewise は「同様に」、introduce は「～を紹介する」、image は「画像、映像」の意味。

⑩ **Although there remain several issues such as setting safety standards, it will not be long before people can drive a flying car.**
  - although は「～けれども」、issue は「問題」、set は「～を定める、設定する」、safety standard は「安全基準」の意味。

READING SKILL 4

Insects: Food for the Future

 読解のポイント　　　　　　　教科書 p.26

1. 昆虫を食べるべき理由とはどのようなものですか。
2. どのような昆虫食品が売られていますか。

Setting **You are reading a website about using insects as food.**

Today, unstable food supply is a serious global issue. ① According to the FAO, there will be a food shortage in the near future because of climate change and population growth. ② In 2013, the FAO suggested one solution to this problem: eating insects.

There are good reasons to eat insects. First, they are nutritious. ③ For example, locusts, crickets, and cicadas are a rich source of protein, iron, and calcium. ④ That is why they have long been eaten in Africa, Latin America, and Asia, including some regions in Japan. ⑤ Second, insects are easy to farm. ⑥ They need far less feed and water than farm animals, and they grow fast. ⑦ Under good conditions, insects can be produced stably regardless of the season.

⑧ Recently, products such as meatballs and protein bars containing insects have appeared in Western countries. ⑨ In Japan, too, cricket crackers are found on store shelves. ⑩ One day, you may see insects on your dining table.

単語・語句の研究

☐ unstable [ʌnstéibl]	形 不安定な、変動しやすい
☐ supply [səplái]	名 供給
☐ FAO [éfèióu]	国際連合食糧農業機関 (Food and Agriculture Organization of the United Nations)
☐ nutritious [njuːtríʃəs]	形 栄養のある　参考 nutrition (栄養)
☐ locust (s) [lóukəst(s)]	名 バッタ、イナゴ

☐ **cricket** [kríkət]	名 コオロギ
☐ **cicada** [sikéidə]	名 セミ
☐ **protein** [próuti:n]	名 たんぱく質
☐ **calcium** [kælsiəm]	名 カルシウム
☐ **Latin America** [lǽtin əmérəkə]	名 ラテンアメリカ、中南米諸国
☐ **stably** [stéibli]	副 安定して　参考 stable（安定した）
☐ **regardless** [rigá:rdləs]	形 無頓着な、気にかけない
☐ regardless of 〜	〜とは関係なく、〜にかかわらず 例 Many people joined our reading club regardless of age or gender. （私たちの読書会には、年齢や性別に関係なく多くの人が参加した）
☐ **meatball (s)** [mí:tbɔ:l(z)]	名 ミートボール、肉だんご
☐ **bar (s)** [bá:r(z)]	名 棒状のかたまり、バー
☐ **cracker (s)** [krǽkər(z)]	名 クラッカー、ビスケット
☐ dining [dáiniŋ]	名 食事

 解説

① **According to the FAO, there will be a food shortage in the near future because of climate change and population growth.**

● according to 〜は「〜によると」、shortage は「不足」、because of 〜は「〜が原因で」、climate change は「気候変動」、population growth は「人口増加」の意味。

② **In 2013, the FAO suggested one solution to this problem: eating insects.**

● suggest は「〜を提案する」、solution は「解決策」、insect は「昆虫」の意味。

③ **For example, locusts, crickets, and cicadas are a rich source of protein, iron, and calcium.**

● source は「源」、iron は「鉄分」の意味。

④ **That is why they have long been eaten in Africa, Latin America, and Asia, including some regions in Japan.**
- that is why ～は「それが～する理由だ、だから～だ」の意味。
- they は locusts, crickets, and cicadas をさす。
- they have long been eaten は現在完了の受け身の文。「それらが長い間食べられてきた」の意味。
- including は「～を含めて」、region は「地域、地方」の意味。

⑤ **Second, insects are easy to farm.**
- easy to ～は「～しやすい」、farm は「～を農場で飼育する」の意味。

⑥ **They need far less feed and water than farm animals, and they grow fast.**
- far は「はるかに、ずっと」の意味で、less「より少ない」を強調している。
- feed は「飼料、えさ」、farm animal は「家畜」の意味。

⑦ **Under good conditions, insects can be produced stably regardless of the season.**
- condition は「条件、状況」の意味。
- produce は「～を生産する」の意味で、ここでは過去分詞になっている。〈can be + 過去分詞〉は「～されることができる（＝～することができる）」という受け身の文。

⑧ **Recently, products such as meatballs and protein bars containing insects have appeared in Western countries.**
- products ～ containing insects がこの文の主語。
- contain は「～を含む、～が入っている」の意味で、ここでは現在分詞になっている。containing insects が products such as meatballs and protein bars を後ろから修飾している。
- appear は「（製品が）発売される」の意味で、ここでは過去分詞になっている。〈have + 過去分詞〉で現在完了の文。

⑨ **In Japan, too, cricket rice crackers are found on store shelves.**
- 受け身の文。
- rice cracker は「せんべい」の意味。
- shelves は shelf「棚」の複数形。

⑩ **One day, you may see insects on your dining table.**
- one day は「ある日」、dining table は「食卓、ダイニングテーブル」の意味。

Dragon Boat Racing

 読解のポイント
1. ドラゴンボートレースのクルーはどのようなメンバーで構成されていますか。
2. 目入れ式はどのような目的で行われますか。

Setting **A student from China is talking about an event.**

① Today, I would like to introduce a popular event in China. ② That is dragon boat racing.

③ First, I'll explain the basic points of the race. ④ Crews on dragon-shaped boats compete with each other along a several-hundred-meter straight course. ⑤ A crew typically consists of twenty paddlers, a drummer, and a steerer. ⑥ The drummer leads the paddlers with a drumbeat, and the steerer controls the boat.

⑦ Second, I'll talk about its historical and cultural aspects. Dragon boat racing originated in China over 2,000 years ago. ⑧ A part of Chinese culture is seen in the Eye Dotting Ceremony held before the race. ⑨ The dragon's eyes on the head of each boat are painted to "awaken" the dragon from its sleep, which is for water safety.

⑩ Today, dragon boat races are held in many countries such as Australia and Japan. ⑪ A traditional Chinese event has now become a modern sport across borders.

ABC 単語・語句の研究

☐ racing [réisiŋ]	名 レース
☐ **typically** [típikli]	副 一般的に
☐ paddler (s) [pǽdlər(z)]	名 漕ぎ手
☐ drummer [drʌ́mər]	名 ドラマー、太鼓奏者
☐ steerer [stíərər]	名 舵取り
	参考 steer（～を操縦する、舵を取る）
☐ drumbeat [drʌ́mbiːt]	名 太鼓の音
☐ originate (d) [ərídʒənèit(id)]	動 生じる、始まる

□ originate in 〜	〜で始まる、〜に起源がある
	例 Halloween originated in ancient Celtic culture.
	（ハロウィーンは古代ケルト文化に起源がある）
□ Eye Dotting Ceremony	目入れ式
□ **dot (ting)** [dát(iŋ)]	動 〜に点を打つ
□ awaken [əwéikən]	動 〜を目覚めさせる、覚醒させる

 解説

① **Today, I would like to introduce a popular event in China.**
- would like to 〜は「〜したいのですが」と丁寧に言う表現。
- introduceは「〜を紹介する」、eventは「イベント、行事」の意味。

② **That is dragon boat racing.**
- Thatは前文のa popular event in Chinaをさす。
- dragon boat racingは「ドラゴンボートレース」の意味。

③ **First, I'll explain the basic points of the race.**
- basicは「基礎の、基本的な」、raceは「レース」の意味。

④ **Crews on dragon-shaped boats compete with each other along a several-hundred-meter straight course.**
- Crews on dragon-shaped boatsがこの文の主語。
- crewは「乗組員、クルー」、dragon-shapedは「ドラゴンの形の」、compete with 〜は「〜と競う」、several-hundred-meterは「数百メートルの」、courseは「コース」の意味。

⑤ **A crew typically consists of twenty paddlers, a drummer, and a steerer.**
- consist of 〜は「〜から成り立つ」の意味。

⑥ **The drummer leads the paddlers with a drumbeat, and the steerer controls the boat.**
- leadは「〜を導く、案内する」、controlは「〜を操作する、コントロールする」の意味。

⑦ **Second, I'll talk about its historical and cultural aspects.**

- historical は「歴史的な」、cultural は「文化的な」、aspect は「側面、面」の意味。

⑧ **A part of Chinese culture is seen in the Eye Dotting Ceremony held before the race.**

- 受け身の文。
- held は過去分詞で、held before the race が the Eye Dotting Ceremony を後ろから修飾している。

✎**確認** ( ) 内に適切な語を入れなさい。

ア. これはフランス人の小説家によって書かれた本だ。

This is a book ( ) ( ) a French novelist.

イ. 私は叔母によって作られたキャンドルに火をつけた。

I lit a candle ( ) ( ) my aunt.

⑨ **The dragon's eyes on the head of each boat are painted to "awaken" the dragon from its sleep, which is for water safety.**

- 受け身の文。
- The dragon's eyes on the head of each boat がこの文の主語。
- to "awaken" the dragon from its sleep は不定詞の副詞的用法で、ドラゴンの目が描かれる目的を表している。
- which は関係代名詞 (非制限用法) で、「そしてそのことは〜」と The dragon's eyes 〜 its sleep の文全体について説明している。

✎**確認** ( ) 内に適切な語を入れなさい。

ア. 彼女は部活動を辞めたが、そのことは私たちを驚かせた。

She quit the club, ( ) ( ) us.

イ. 彼は子どもの頃に海外に住んでおり、そのことが留学の際に役立った。

He lived abroad as a child, ( ) ( ) him when he studied abroad.

⑩ **Today, dragon boat races are held in many countries such as Australia and Japan.**

- 受け身の文。

⑪ **A traditional Chinese event has now become a modern sport across borders.**

- 現在完了〈has + 過去分詞〉の文。
- across borders は「国境を越えて」の意味。

READING SKILL 6

Placebo Effects

 読解のポイント

1. プラシーボ効果とは具体的にどのような現象ですか。
2. どのような実験が行われましたか。

Setting **You are reading a magazine article about psychology.**

① The placebo effect is a well-known psychological phenomenon. A placebo is fake medicine. ② Patients who are treated with a placebo sometimes feel cured because they believe it is "real" medicine. ③ This phenomenon shows that the mind and body are closely connected. ④ The placebo effect has been confirmed in medical science as well as in psychology.

⑤ In one experiment, a researcher divided people into two groups and asked them to drink the same vanilla milkshakes. ⑥ At the time, the researcher explained to one group that the milkshakes had an extremely high number of calories. ⑦ To the other group, the researcher said that the milkshakes were healthy. ⑧ As a result of this experiment, it was found that the former group felt less hungry than the latter group did. ⑨ The researcher concluded that people's beliefs led to a change in the reactions of their bodies.

⑩ The placebo effect may happen to anybody, especially to those who tend to take things seriously. It shows the power of the mind over the body.

単語・語句の研究

□ placebo [pləsí:bou]	名 偽薬、プラシーボ	
□ psychological [sàikəládʒikl]	形 心理学の	
□ phenomenon [finámənàn]	名 現象、事象	
□ fake [féik]	形 にせの	
□ closely [klóusli]	副 密接に **参考** close（密接な）	
□ confirm (ed) [kənfə́ːrm(d)]	動 ～を（本当だと）確かめる	
□ psychology [saikálədʒi]	名 心理学	

☐ divide ~ into ...	～を…に分ける 例 I divided the pizza into eight equal parts.（私はピザを 8 等分した）
☐ milkshake (s) [mílkʃèik(s)]	名 ミルクシェイク
☐ **calorie (s)** [kǽləri(z)]	名 カロリー
☐ the former ~, the latter ~	前者は～、後者は～ 例 We have a dog and a cat. The former is black, and the latter is white.（私たちは犬と猫を飼っている。前者は黒色で、後者は白色だ）
☐ latter [lǽtər]	形 （2 つのうち）後者の
☐ **reaction (s)** [riǽkʃn(z)]	名 反応　参考 react（反応する）

 解説

① **The placebo effect is a well-known psychological phenomenon.**
- placebo effect は「プラシーボ効果」、well-known は「よく知られている、有名な」の意味。

② **Patients who are treated with a placebo sometimes feel cured because they believe it is "real" medicine.**
- Patients who are treated with a placebo がこの文の主語。
- who は関係代名詞で、who are treated with a placebo が先行詞 Patients を後ろから修飾している。
- patient は「患者、病人」の意味。
- treat ~ with ... は「…で～を治療する」の意味で、ここでは受け身。
- cure は「～を治療する」の意味で、ここでは過去分詞になっている。

③ **This phenomenon shows that the mind and body are closely connected.**
- This phenomenon は②の内容全体をさす。
- that は接続詞で、show that ~ は「～ということを示す」の意味。
- mind は「心、精神」、connected は「関連した」の意味。

④ **The placebo effect has been confirmed in medical science as well as in psychology.**

- 〈has been + 過去分詞〉は現在完了の受け身の文。
- medical scienceは「医学」、~ as well as ...は「…だけでなく~も」の意味。

⑤ **In one experiment, a researcher divided people into two groups and asked them to drink the same vanilla milkshakes.**

- 〈ask + O + to + 動詞の原形〉は「Oに~するように頼む」の意味。
- vanillaは「バニラ味の」の意味。

⑥ **At the time, the researcher explained to one group that the milkshakes had an extremely high number of calories.**

- at the timeは「そのとき」、extremelyは「とても、きわめて」の意味。
- thatは接続詞で、explain to ~ that ...は「~に…ということを説明する」の意味。

⑦ **To the other group, the researcher said that the milkshakes were healthy.**

- the other groupは「もう1つのグループ」の意味で、2つのグループのうち、⑥のone groupとは別のグループということ。
- thatは接続詞で、say that ~は「~ということを言う」の意味。

⑧ **As a result of this experiment, it was found that the former group felt less hungry than the latter group did.**

- itは形式主語で、真の主語はthat節 (that the former group ~ the latter group did) である。
- the former groupは⑥、the latter groupは⑦のグループをさす。
- lessは「より~でなく」の意味。
- didは代動詞で、feltの代わりに使われている。

⑨ **The researcher concluded that people's beliefs led to a change in the reactions of their bodies.**

- thatは接続詞で、conclude that ~は「~と結論を下す」の意味。

⑩ **The placebo effect may happen to anybody, especially to those who tend to take things seriously.**

- happen to ~は「~に起こる」、tend to ~は「~する傾向がある」、take things seriouslyは「物事を深刻に受けとめる」の意味。
- those whoはthose people whoと考えて、whoは関係代名詞。

Magawa: The Mine-Detecting Rat

 読解のポイント

1. なぜネズミは地雷を発見する仕事に向いているのですか。
2. マガワはキャリア全体でどれくらいの働きをしましたか。

Setting **You are reading a website about a rat that worked for peace.**

① Magawa was a giant pouched rat which could detect landmines. He was born in 2013 in Tanzania, Africa. ② He was trained to find landmines together with other rats. ③ The rats are suitable for the job because they are good at smelling. ④ They are also light enough to walk over minefields without setting off the landmines.

⑤ In 2016, he was sent to Cambodia, where he helped humans safely remove landmines. ⑥ Compared with other skilled rats, Magawa was a standout sniffer. ⑦ In his career, he helped clear the area about the size of 31 soccer fields. He found 71 landmines and 38 unexploded bombs. ⑧ Magawa is believed to have saved many lives in Cambodia.

⑨ Because of his great contribution to peace, he was awarded a gold medal for animals by a UK charity association in 2020. ⑩ He was the first rat that received this special honor. It is amazing that such a small animal could help so many people.

ABC 単語・語句の研究

☐ **Magawa** [məgáːwə]	图 マガワ((ネズミの名前))
☐ **detect (ing)** [ditékt(iŋ)]	動 〜を見つける
☐ **pouch (ed)** [páutʃ(t)]	動 〜を袋に入れる
☐ **suitable** [súːtəbl]	形 適した、ふさわしい
☐ **minefield (s)** [máinfiːld(z)]	图 地雷原
☐ **set off 〜**	〜を爆発させる 例 At the moment, someone set off a bomb. (その瞬間、何者かが爆弾を爆発させた)
☐ **standout** [stǽndàut]	形 優れた、すばらしい

□	sniffer [snífər]	名 かぐ人［者］、（爆発物の）捜索動物
□	unexploded [ʌniksplóudid]	形 爆発していない
□	association [əsòusiéiʃn]	名 団体、協会

 解説

① **Magawa was a giant pouched rat which could detect landmines.**
- which は関係代名詞で、which could detect landmines が先行詞 a giant pouched rat を後ろから修飾している。
- giant pouched rat は「アフリカオニネズミ」、landmine は「地雷」の意味。

② **He was trained to find landmines together with other rats.**
- He は①の Magawa をさす。
- train 〜 to ... は「〜を…するように訓練する」の意味で、ここでは受け身になっている。

③ **The rats are suitable for the job because they are good at smelling.**
- the job は地雷を発見する仕事のこと。
- smell は「においをかぐ」の意味で、ここでは動名詞になっている。

④ **They are also light enough to walk over minefields without setting off the landmines.**
- They は③の The rats をさす。
- 〈形容詞＋ enough to ＋動詞の原形〉は「十分…なので〜できる、〜するのに十分…だ」の意味。

⑤ **In 2016, he was sent to Cambodia, where he helped humans safely remove landmines.**
- he は Magawa をさす。
- 過去の受け身の文。
- Cambodia は「カンボジア（（国名））」、remove は「〜を取り除く、除去する」の意味。
- where は関係副詞で、「そしてそこで〜」と Cambodia について説明している。
- 〈help ＋ O ＋動詞の原形〉は「O が〜するのを助ける」の意味。

⑥ **Compared with other skilled rats, Magawa was a standout sniffer.**
- compared with ～は「～と比べて」、skilled は「熟練した、技術のある」の意味。

⑦ **In his career, he helped clear the area about the size of 31 soccer fields.**
- 〈help + 動詞の原形〉で「～するのに役立つ」の意味。
- the size of 31 soccer fields は「サッカー場31面分の広さ」の意味。

⑧ **Magawa is believed to have saved many lives in Cambodia.**
- ～ is believed to ... は「～は…すると信じられている」の意味。
- to have saved は不定詞の完了形で、「～を救った」の意味。
- lives は「人、人命」の意味。

⑨ **Because of his great contribution to peace, he was awarded a gold medal for animals by a UK charity association in 2020.**
- contribution to ～は「～への貢献」、gold medal は「金メダル」、charity association は「慈善団体」の意味。
- 〈award + O_1 + O_2〉は「O_1 に O_2 を (賞として) 与える」の意味で、ここでは受け身になっている。

⑩ **He was the first rat that received this special honor.**
- that は関係代名詞で、that 以下が先行詞 the first rat を後ろから修飾している。先行詞に first などの序数詞がついているときは、関係代名詞はふつう that を使う。
- honor は「栄誉」の意味で、this special honor は前文の a gold medal for animals by a UK charity association をさす。

A Reassuring Song

 読解のポイント　　　　　　　　　　　教科書 p.44
1. "ArtistsCAN" はどのようなプロジェクトですか。
2. "Lean On Me" の重要なメッセージとは何ですか。

Setting **You are reading a blog about memorable songs.**

① In April 2020, "Lean On Me" was sung by "ArtistsCAN" as a part of the COVID-19 relief effort in Canada. ② ArtistsCAN consisted of 27 Canadian singers, who sang part by part online. ③ The purpose of this project was to support people who fought against the coronavirus pandemic.

④ The song was originally sung by Bill Withers and became a big hit in the US in 1972. ⑤ Ever since, many artists have covered it on occasions where people need support.

⑥ The song has a key message: it is important for people to understand each other's weaknesses and provide mutual support. ⑦ For example, some people may feel relieved to hear the lyrics "Sometimes in our lives we all have pain." ⑧ Others may be reassured by the words "Lean on me when you're not strong." ⑨ "Lean On Me" is a song that encourages people in difficult times.

🅰🅱🅲 単語・語句の研究

☐ reassuring [rìːəʃúəriŋ]	形 安心させる、元気づける
☐ lean [líːn]	動 寄りかかる、もたれる
☐ lean on ～	～に頼る 例 He needs someone to lean on. （彼にはだれか頼れる人が必要だ）
☐ COVID-19 [kóuvidnàintíːn]	名 新型コロナウイルス感染症
☐ relief [rilíːf]	名 救済、救援
☐ part by part	パートごとに
☐ coronavirus [kəróunəvàirəs]	名 コロナウイルス
☐ pandemic [pændémik]	名 世界的流行、パンデミック

□ Bill Withers [bíl wíðərz]	图 ビル・ウィザーズ((人名))
□ **weakness (es)** [wíːknəs(iz)]	图 弱点、欠点
□ **lyric (s)** [lírik(s)]	图 歌詞
□ **reassure (d)** [riːəʃúər(d)]	動 ～を安心させる、元気づかせる

 解説

① **In April 2020, "Lean On Me" was sung by "ArtistsCAN" as a part of the COVID-19 relief effort in Canada.**
- 過去の受け身の文。〈was + 過去分詞 + by ...〉は「…によって～された」の意味。sung は sing「～を歌う」の過去分詞。
- "Lean On Me"「リーン・オン・ミー」は曲名。"ArtistsCAN"「アーティスツ・キャン」はカナダ出身の歌手タイラー・ショーが立ち上げたプロジェクトの名前。
- relief effort は「救援活動」の意味。

② **ArtistsCAN consisted of 27 Canadian singers, who sang part by part online.**
- consist of ～は「～から成り立つ」、Canadian は「カナダ人の」、online は「オンラインで」の意味。
- who は関係代名詞で、「そしてその人たちは～」と 27 Canadian singers について説明している。
- ArtistsCAN には、カナダ出身のジャスティン・ビーバーやアヴリル・ラヴィーンも参加した。

③ **The purpose of this project was to support people who fought against the coronavirus pandemic.**
- purpose は「目的」、fight against ～は「～と戦う」の意味。
- to support は不定詞の名詞的用法。
- who は関係代名詞で、who 以下が先行詞 people を後ろから修飾している。
- 《確認》 (　) 内に適切な語を入れなさい。
  - ア．彼女はロンドンで活動する日本人歌手だ。
    She is a Japanese (　　　) (　　　) works in London.
  - イ．野球部に入りたい人はたくさんいる。
    There are a lot of people (　　　) (　　　) to join the baseball team.

④ **The song was originally sung by Bill Withers and became a big hit in the US in 1972.**
- originally は「もともと」、big hit は「大ヒット曲」の意味。

⑤ **Ever since, many artists have covered it on occasions where people need support.**
- ever since は「それ以来(ずっと)」、cover は「〜をカバーする、〜のカバーバージョンを作る」、occasion は「時、場合」の意味。
- it は④の The song、つまり "Lean On Me" をさす。
- where は関係副詞で、where 以下が occasions を後ろから修飾している。先行詞が状況や立場、事情、事例を表す語の場合も関係副詞 where が用いられる。

🖊 **確認**　(　　)内に適切な語を入れなさい。

ア．大きな貧富の差がある状況は改善されていない。

The situation (　　　) (　　　) is a large wealth gap between the rich and the poor has not improved.

イ．これらのルールが当てはまらない場合も多くある。

There are many cases (　　) these (　　) do not apply.

⑥ **The song has a key message: it is important for people to understand each other's weaknesses and provide mutual support.**
- :(コロン)は後ろに語句や文を置いて、説明や例示をするのに使われる。ここでは、a key message「重要なメッセージ」の具体的な内容が示されている。

⑦ **For example, some people may feel relieved to hear the lyrics "Sometimes in our lives we all have pain."**
- relieved は「ほっとした、安心の」、pain は「苦しみ」の意味。
- lives は life「人生」の複数形。

⑧ **Others may be reassured by the words "Lean on me when you're not strong."**
- Others は⑦の some people と対になっている。Some people 〜. Others .... は「〜する人もいれば、…する人もいる」の意味。

⑨ **"Lean On Me" is a song that encourages people in difficult times.**
- that は関係代名詞で、that 以下が先行詞 a song を後ろから修飾している。
- encourage は「〜を励ます、元気づける」、difficult は「つらい、困難な」の意味。

UNIT 2

Lesson 1-7

"Priceless" Cafe, "Priceless" Community

 読解のポイント

教科書 p.52 *l*.1〜p.52 *l*.13

1. ComeUnity Cafeとはどのようなカフェですか。
2. "Pay-What-You-Can" systemとはどのような仕組みですか。

Setting **A unique cafe is introduced in a newspaper.**

① In Tennessee the US, there is a cafe named ComeUnity Cafe. ② The cafe differs from others because it does not have set prices, adopting a "Pay-What-You-Can" system. ③ This means that customers decide how much they pay, depending on their financial circumstances and goodwill.

④ For example, a person with enough money might pay 20 dollars for a lunch worth 11 dollars. ⑤ The extra nine dollars becomes a donation to the cafe. ⑥ On the other hand, a person who cannot afford the lunch might work in the cafe as a volunteer. ⑦ One-hour of work compensates for one free meal. ⑧ Moreover, if people work for two hours, they can wash and dry their clothes in the laundry room. ⑨ This offer helps those who do not have a washing machine at home.

🅐🅑🅒 単語・語句の研究

☐ priceless [práisləs]	形 値踏みのできない、たいへん貴重な 参考 price(価格、値段)、-less(〜の及ばない)
☐ Tennessee [tènəsíː]	名 テネシー州((アメリカ南東部の州))
☐ ComeUnity [kʌmjúːnəti]	コミュニティ((community「共同体」と come「来る」+ unity「調和」をかけたカフェの名前))
☐ **differ(s)** [dífər(z)]	動 異なる、違う 参考 different(異なった、違った)
☐ differ from 〜	〜と異なる 例 Their culture differs from ours.(彼らの文化は私たちの文化と異なる)

UNIT 2

☐ **adopt(ing)** [ədápt(iŋ)]	動 ～を採用する
☐ **"Pay-What-You-Can" system**	客が価格を決定する仕組み
☐ **financial** [fənǽnʃl]	形 金融上の、経済的な 参考 finance（財務、金融）
☐ **goodwill** [gùdwíl]	名 善意、好意
☐ **afford** [əfɔ́ːrd]	動 ～する（経済的な）余裕がある
☐ **compensate(s)** [kámpənsèit(s)]	動 埋め合わせをする、補う
☐ **compensate for ～**	～の埋め合わせをする 例 Long naps can compensate for lack of sleep. （長い昼寝をすると睡眠不足を補うことができる）

解説

① **In Tennessee the US, there is a cafe named ComeUnity Cafe.**
- named は「～と名づけられた」という意味の過去分詞で、named ComeUnity Cafe が a cafe を後ろから修飾している。
- 確認 （　）内に適切な語を入れなさい。
  - ア．彼はココという名前の猫を飼っている。
    He has a cat (　　　) Coco.
  - イ．これらはどら焼きと呼ばれる日本のお菓子だ。
    These are Japanese sweets (　　　) *dorayaki*.

② **The cafe differs from others because it does not have set prices, adopting a "Pay-What-You-Can" system.**
- 分詞構文。adopting a "Pay-What-You-Can" system の部分が it does not have set prices の理由を説明している。
- 確認 （　）内に適切な語を入れなさい。
  - ア．お金がないので、私はその車を買うことができない。
    (　　　) no money, I can't buy the car.
  - イ．お腹が空いているので、彼女は今昼食を食べたいと思っている。
    (　　　) hungry, she wants to have lunch now.

③ **This means that customers decide how much they pay, depending on their financial circumstances and goodwill.**
- how much they pay が decide の目的語になっている間接疑問文。〈how much + S + V〉で「Sがいくら〜するか」という意味。
- *⃝確認* （　　）内に適切な語を入れなさい。
  ア．私は趣味にいくらお金を費やしたかわからない。
  　　I don't know (　　　) (　　　) I have spent on my hobby.
  イ．あなたは部屋に何人いたかを覚えていますか。
  　　Do you remember (　　　) (　　　) people there were in the room?

④ **For example, a person with enough money might pay 20 dollars for a lunch worth 11 dollars.**
- a person with enough money がこの文の主語。
- a lunch worth 11 dollars は「11ドルの価値があるランチ」の意味。

⑤ **The extra nine dollars becomes a donation to the cafe.**
- extra は「余計な、余分の」、donation は「寄付」の意味。

⑥ **On the other hand, a person who cannot afford the lunch might work in the cafe as a volunteer.**
- on the other hand は「一方で」の意味。④の例との対比になっている。
- a person who cannot afford the lunch がこの文の主語。

⑦ **One-hour of work compensates for one free meal.**
- free は「無料の」、meal は「食事」の意味。

⑧ **Moreover, if people work for two hours, they can wash and dry their clothes in the laundry room.**
- moreover は「その上、さらに」と情報を付け加える表現。

⑨ **This offer helps those who do not have a washing machine at home.**
- those who do not have a washing machine at home が helps の目的語になっている。

読解のポイント

1. クレンショーさんはどのようなきっかけでComeUnity Cafeを始めましたか。
2. ComeUnity Cafeは町の人々にとってどのような存在ですか。

UNIT 2

ComeUnity Cafe was opened by Amy Crenshaw in 2013. ① She used to be a nurse. ② After her marriage, she devoted herself to raising ten children: three biological and seven adopted from China and Ethiopia. ③ One day, Crenshaw heard from her oldest daughter about a cafe in Colorado with the "Pay-What-You-Can" system. ④ Inspired by this idea, she decided to start such a cafe in her town. She thought it was her calling.

⑤ Crenshaw's motto is "to love, to feed, to dignify." ⑥ With this in mind, she serves healthy meals to all, including those who have no money. ⑦ For these meals, she uses organic and seasonal ingredients. ⑧ Some of them are products grown in her garden. ⑨ She also often uses fresh vegetables donated by local farmers and suppliers. ⑩ They are great supporters of what she does.

ComeUnity Cafe has about 50 seats, and they are always occupied. ⑪ As its name shows, the cafe unites people who come to the cafe, regardless of how much money they have. ⑫ ComeUnity Cafe is not only a "priceless" cafe but also a "priceless" community for everyone in town.

🅐🅑🅒 単語・語句の研究

☐ **Amy Crenshaw** [éimi krènʃɔ:] 图エイミー・クレンショー((人名))

☐ **marriage** [mǽridʒ] 图結婚
　　　　　　　　　　　　　　参考 marry (〜と結婚する)

☐ **devote(d)** [divóut(id)] 動〜をささげる

☐ devote *oneself* to 〜 〜に一身をささげる、専念する
　　　　　　　　　　　　　　例 He devoted himself to his research.
　　　　　　　　　　　　　　(彼は研究に専念した)

☐ **biological** [bàiəládʒikl] 形生物学上の
　　　　　　　　　　　　　　参考 biology (生物学)

☐ Ethiopia [ìːθióupiə]	图 エチオピア((アフリカ東部の国))
☐ Colorado [kàlərædou]	图 コロラド州((アメリカ中西部の州))
☐ **calling** [kɔ́ːliŋ]	图 天職
☐ dignify [dígnəfài]	動 ～に威厳をつける、尊くする
☐ with ～ in mind	～を念頭に置いて、考慮に入れて 例 This app is designed with color-blind users in mind. (このアプリは色覚障がいのあるユーザーを考慮してデザインされている)
☐ **organic** [ɔːrɡǽnik]	形 有機栽培の、有機飼育の
☐ supplier(s) [səpláiər(z)]	图 供給者、納入業者 参考 supply(～を供給する)
☐ **occupied** [ákjəpàid] < **occupy**	動 ～を占有する、使用する
☐ **unite(s)** [junáit(s)]	動 ～を結びつける、団結させる 参考 united(連合した、合併した)

 解説

① **She used to be a nurse.**
- used to ～は「かつては～だった」の意味。

② **After her marriage, she devoted herself to raising ten children: three biological and seven adopted from China and Ethiopia.**
- :(コロン)は後ろに語句や文を置いて、補足説明をしたり例を示したりするために使われる。ここでは、クレンショーさんの10人の子どもたちのうち、3人は自分が産んだ子どもで、7人が養子であることが説明されている。
- raiseは「～を育てる」、adoptedは「養子になった」の意味。

③ **One day, Crenshaw heard from her oldest daughter about a cafe in Colorado with the "Pay-What-You-Can" system.**
- a cafe in Colorado with the "Pay-What-You-Can" systemが前置詞about の目的語になっている。

④ **Inspired by this idea, she decided to start such a cafe in her town.**

- 過去分詞 inspired の前に Being が省略されている分詞構文。「このアイディアに影響を受けて、そして〜」と付帯状況を表している。受け身を表す分詞構文は〈being ＋過去分詞〉の形になるが、being が文頭にくる場合はふつう being を省略する。
- 確認 （　　）内に適切な語を入れなさい。
  ア．五稜郭は上から見ると星型に見える。
  （　　　） from above, Goryokaku Fort looks star-shaped.
  イ．薄い文字で書かれていたので、そのメモは読みづらかった。
  （　　　） in thin letters, the note was difficult to read.

⑤ **Crenshaw's motto is "to love, to feed, to dignify."**

- motto は「座右の銘、モットー」の意味。ここでは、be動詞の後ろに補語として3つの不定詞（"to love, to feed, to dignify"）が並んでいて、「クレンショーのモットーは『愛すること』、『食事を与えること』、『尊ぶこと』である」という意味の文である。
- feed は「〜に食べ物を与える、〜を養う」の意味。

⑥ **With this in mind, she serves healthy meals to all, including those who have no money.**

- serve は「（食事）を出す」、including は「〜を含めて」の意味。

⑦ **For these meals, she uses organic and seasonal ingredients.**

- seasonal は「季節の」、ingredient は「材料」の意味。

⑧ **Some of them are products grown in her garden.**

- them は前文の organic and seasonal ingredients をさす。
- 過去分詞の grown 以下が products を後ろから修飾している。

⑨ **She also often uses fresh vegetables donated by local farmers and suppliers.**

- fresh vegetables 以下が uses の目的語。過去分詞の donated 以下が fresh vegetables を後ろから修飾している。

⑩ **They are great supporters of what she does.**
- このwhatは関係代名詞。〈what + S + V〉で「Sが〜すること［もの］」という意味。what she doesは直訳すると「彼女がすること」だが、「彼女の活動」をさしている。
- 🖊️確認 （　）内に適切な語を入れなさい。
  - ア．私の一日の食事をお見せします。
    - I'll show you （　　　） （　　　） eat in a day.
  - イ．私は彼の言葉が聞こえなかった。
    - I didn't hear （　　　） （　　　） said.

⑪ **As its name shows, the cafe unites people who come to the cafe, regardless of how much money they have.**
- ここでのasは「〜の通り」という意味の接続詞。
- whoは主格の関係代名詞で、who come to the cafeが先行詞peopleを修飾している。
- regardless of 〜は「〜にかかわらず、関係なく」の意味。
- how much money they haveは「彼らがどれくらいお金を持っているか」という意味の間接疑問文。

⑫ **ComeUnity Cafe is not only a "priceless" cafe but also a "priceless" community for everyone in town.**
- not only 〜 but also ... は「〜だけでなく…も」の意味。
- "priceless" cafeのpricelessは「値段のない」の意味で使われており、"priceless" communityのpricelessは「たいへん貴重な」の意味で使われている。

確認問題

1 下線部の発音が同じものには○、違うものには×を ( ) に書き入れなさい。

(1) di<u>ff</u>er ― b<u>i</u>ological ( )

(2) f<u>ee</u>d ― m<u>ea</u>l ( )

(3) dev<u>o</u>te ― Ethi<u>o</u>pia ( )

(4) don<u>a</u>tion ― m<u>a</u>rriage ( )

(5) aff<u>or</u>d ― <u>or</u>ganic ( )

2 ☐ から最も適切な語を選び、( ) に書き入れなさい。

(1) Their team ( ) a new approach.

(2) My grandparents helped me with ( ) support.

(3) She realized that her ( ) was to protect marine life.

(4) Some famous guests were invited to ( ) the ceremony.

(5) We are the largest ( ) of smartphones in this country.

calling	dignify	supplier	adopted	financial

3 日本語に合うように、( ) 内に適切な語を入れなさい。

(1) 彼は生物学上の父親をさがしていた。

He was looking for his ( ) father.

(2) その店は有機野菜を売っている。

The shop sells ( ) vegetables.

(3) 私は彼らの好意に応えたい。

I want to return their ( ).

(4) そのレストランは満席だった。

All seats were ( ) at the restaurant.

(5) その美術館を訪れて、たいへん貴重な芸術作品を見るべきだ。

You should visit the art museum and see ( ) works of art.

4 日本語に合うように、（　　）内に適切な語を入れなさい。

(1) このシステムは安全性を念頭に置いて作られた。

This system was created with safety (　　　　) (　　　　).

(2) 彼女は仕事に一身をささげた。

She (　　　　) (　　　　) to her job.

(3) アメリカでは法律は州ごとに異なる。

In the US, laws (　　　　) (　　　　) state to state.

(4) 努力で経験不足を補うことができる。

Hard work can (　　　　) (　　　　) lack of experience.

(5) ここにはかつてデパートがあった。

There (　　　　) (　　　　) be a department store here.

5 次の英語を日本語に訳しなさい。

(1) Surprised at the news, they became quiet.

_____

(2) Having a lot of homework, I won't watch TV tonight.

_____

(3) Let's count the number of those who can come to the party.

_____

6 日本語に合うように、[　　] 内の語を並べかえなさい。

(1) 彼らにはリリーという名前の娘がいる。

They [named / a / Lily / have / daughter].

They _____.

(2) この村に住んでいる人々には車が必要だ。

Cars are [who / for / live / those / necessary] in this village.

Cars are _____ in this village.

(3) 彼がお年玉にいくらもらったのか私は知らない。

I don't [got / how / he / know / much] for his New Year's gift.

I don't _____ for his New Year's gift.

7 次の英文を読み、設問に答えなさい。

In Tennessee the US, there is a cafe named ComeUnity Cafe. The cafe differs from others because it does not have set prices, ①(adopt) a "Pay-What-You-Can" system. This means that customers decide how much they pay, depending on their financial circumstances and goodwill. ②( ), a person with enough money might pay 20 dollars for a lunch worth 11 dollars. The extra nine dollars becomes a donation to the cafe. ③On ( ), a person who cannot afford the lunch might work in the cafe as a volunteer. One-hour of work compensates for one free meal. ④( ), if people work for two hours, they can wash and dry their clothes in the laundry room. ⑤This offer helps those who do not have a washing machine at home.

(1) ①の単語を適切な形に直しなさい。

——————————————

(2) 空所②④に入る最も適切な語句をそれぞれ選び、記号で答えなさい。

　　ア．By mistake　　　イ．As a result
　　ウ．Moreover　　　エ．For example
　　②(　　　)　　④(　　　)

(3) 下線部③が「一方で、ランチのお金を支払う余裕のない人は、ボランティアとしてカフェで働くかもしれない。」という意味になるように、空所に当てはまる3語の英語を書きなさい。

——————————— ——————————— ———————————

(4) 下線部⑤を日本語に訳しなさい。

————————————————————————

(5) 本文の内容に合うように、次の質問に英語で答えなさい。

How many hours do people need to work to wash and dry their clothes in the laundry room?

————————————————————————

8 次の英文を読み、設問に答えなさい。

Crenshaw's motto is "to love, to feed, to dignify." With this in ①( ), she serves healthy meals to all, including those who have no money. For these meals, she uses organic and seasonal ingredients. Some of them are products ②(grow) in her garden. ③ She also often uses fresh vegetables donated by local farmers and suppliers. They are great supporters of what she does.

ComeUnity Cafe has about 50 seats, and they are always ④(occupy). As its name shows, the cafe unites people who come to the cafe, ⑤regardless of [money / have / much / they / how]. ComeUnity Cafe is not only a "priceless" cafe but also a "priceless" community for everyone in town.

(1) 空所①に入る最も適切な語を選び、記号で答えなさい。
    ア．heart　　イ．mind　　ウ．hand　　エ．head　　　　（　　　）
(2) ②の単語を適切な形に直しなさい。
    _____
(3) 下線部③を日本語に訳しなさい。
    _____
(4) ④の単語を適切な形に直しなさい。
    _____
(5) 下線部⑤が「彼らがどれくらいのお金を持っているかにかかわらず」という意味になるように、[　]内の語を並べかえなさい。
    regardless of _____
(6) 本文の内容に合うように、次の質問に英語で答えなさい。
    How many seats does ComeUnity Cafe have?
    _____

Nihonium — A New Element Born in Japan

 読解のポイント

1. ニホニウムはどこで発見されましたか。
2. 元素とはどのようなものですか。

Setting **A new element is featured in a science magazine.**

① In 2017, a new element was officially added to the periodic table of elements. ② It is nihonium (Nh). ③ Nihonium is unique because it is the first element found outside of Western countries. ④ It was discovered in Japan by a researcher, Morita Kosuke, and his team. ⑤ The element was named after the place where it was found, *Nihon*.

⑥ An element is a basic substance that composes things in the world. ⑦ Hydrogen (H), oxygen (O), and carbon (C) are examples of such elements. ⑧ All the elements naturally existing in this world had been found by the middle of the 20th century. ⑨ Since then, scientists have been trying to create a new element artificially.

ⒶⒷⒸ 単語・語句の研究

☐ nihonium [nihóuniəm]	名 ニホニウム ((元素名))
☐ the periodic table of elements	元素周期表
☐ periodic [pìəriádik]	形 周期的な 参考 period (周期)
☐ name ~ after ...	…にちなんで~と名づける 例 We named our daughter Emma after my mother. (私たちは私の母の名前をとって、娘をエマと名づけた)
☐ **compose (s)** [kəmpóuz(iz)]	動 ~を構成する
☐ artificially [à:rtəfíʃəli]	副 人工的に 参考 artificial (人工の、人工的な)

UNIT 2

解説

① **In 2017, a new element was officially added to the periodic table of elements.**
- officially は「正式に、公式に」の意味。
- add ～ to ... は「…に～を加える」の意味で、ここでは受け身になっている。

② **It is nihonium (Nh).**
- Nh はニホニウムの元素記号。

③ **Nihonium is unique because it is the first element found outside of Western countries.**
- unique は「独特の、珍しい」の意味。
- it は Nihonium をさす。
- found は過去分詞で、found outside of Western countries が the first element を後ろから修飾している。
- outside of ～は「～の外で」、Western は「西洋の、欧米の」の意味。

④ **It was discovered in Japan by a researcher, Morita Kosuke, and his team.**
- 受け身の文。〈was + 過去分詞 + by ...〉で「…によって～された」の意味。
- discover は「～を発見する」の意味。
- It は③の Nihonium をさす。

⑤ **The element was named after the place where it was found, *Nihon*.**
- where は関係副詞で、where it was found が先行詞 the place を後ろから修飾している。〈場所 + where + S + V〉で「S が～する場所」の意味。
- 確認　（　　）内に適切な語を入れなさい。
  - ア．ここは私が生まれた病院だ。
    This is the hospital (　　) (　　) was born.
  - イ．私は彼が晩年を過ごした町を訪れた。
    I visited the town (　　) (　　) spent his last years.
- the place where it was found と *Nihon* は同格の関係。
- it は The element、つまり Nihonium をさす。

⑥ **An element is a basic substance that composes things in the world.**
- substanceは「物質」の意味。
- thatは関係代名詞で、that composes things in the worldが先行詞a basic substanceを後ろから修飾している。

⑦ **Hydrogen (H), oxygen (O), and carbon (C) are examples of such elements.**
- hydrogenは「水素」、oxygenは「酸素」、carbonは「炭素」の意味。
- H、O、Cはそれぞれ水素、酸素、炭素の元素記号。

⑧ **All the elements naturally existing in this world had been found by the middle of the 20th century.**
- All the elements naturally existing in this worldがこの文の主語。
- naturallyは「自然に」の意味。
- existingはexist「存在する」の現在分詞で、naturally existing in this worldがAll the elementsを後ろから修飾している。
- 〈had been + 過去分詞〉は過去完了の受け身で、「(ある過去の時点までに)～された」の意味。
- このbyは「～までに」の意味。

⑨ **Since then, scientists have been trying to create a new element artificially.**
- 〈have[has] been + 動詞のing形〉は現在完了進行形で、「(ずっと)～し続けている」の意味。
- 確認 (　)内に適切な語を入れなさい。
  - ア．私たちは子どもの頃から柔道を練習している。
    We (　　) (　　) practicing judo since we were children.
  - イ．ミリーは3時間ずっと勉強している。
    Millie (　　) (　　) studying for three hours.
- try to ～は「～しようとする」の意味。

読解のポイント

1. 森田氏のチームがニホニウムをつくり出すまで何年かかりましたか。
2. ニホニウムの発見はどのような影響をもたらすでしょうか。

① Nihonium was synthesized by the collision of two elements, zinc (Zn) and bismuth (Bi), at an ultrahigh speed in a special machine. ② Morita's team started the experiment to produce the new element in 2003, and it was in 2012 that they finally found clear evidence of successful synthesis. ③ During the nine years, they repeated the experiment about 400 trillion times, and they were able to create their target three times.

④ Nihonium is not a stable element and can exist only for two milliseconds. ⑤ Therefore, it is not considered to provide direct benefits for people's daily lives. ⑥ However, exploring elements offers fundamental knowledge about the world itself. ⑦ This knowledge is essential for scientists to conduct more practical research.

⑧ Morita says, "We named the new element 'nihonium' to thank people in Japan for their support. ⑨ We hope that they will be proud of Japan and be interested in science when they see nihonium on the periodic table. ⑩ We will be happy if that leads to the development of science and technology in Japan in the future."

Ａ Ｂ Ｃ 単語・語句の研究

☐ synthesize (d) [sínθəsàiz(d)]	動 ～を合成する	
☐ collision [kəlíʒn]	名 衝突	
☐ zinc [zíŋk]	名 亜鉛 ((元素名))	
☐ bismuth [bízməθ]	名 ビスマス、蒼鉛 ((元素名))	
☐ ultrahigh [λltrəhái]	形 きわめて高い 参考 ultra-(極端に～、超～)	
☐ evidence [évədns]	名 証拠、根拠	
☐ synthesis [sínθəsis]	名 合成	

☐ **trillion** [tríljən]	图 1兆 参考 million（100万）、billion（10億）
☐ **target** [tá:rgət]	图 対象、目標
☐ **millisecond (s)** [mílisèkənd(z)]	图 ミリセカンド、1000分の1秒 参考 milli-（～の1000分の1）
☐ **therefore** [ðéərfɔ̀:r]	副 それゆえに、したがって
☐ **be considered to ～**	～すると考えられる、みなされる 例 Ladybugs are considered to be a symbol of good luck. （テントウムシは幸運の象徴だとみなされている）
☐ **direct** [dərékt]	形 直接の 参考 indirect（間接の、間接的な）
☐ **fundamental** [fÀndəméntl]	形 基本的な、基礎となる
☐ **practical** [prǽktikl]	形 実用的な
☐ **thank ～ for ...**	…について～に感謝する 例 I thank my classmates for their help. （私はクラスメイトの協力に感謝している）

 解説

① **Nihonium was synthesized by the collision of two elements, zinc (Zn) and bismuth (Bi), at an ultrahigh speed in a special machine.**

● two elements と zinc (Zn) and bismuth (Bi) は同格の関係。

● Zn、Bi はそれぞれ亜鉛、ビスマスの元素記号。

② **Morita's team started the experiment to produce the new element in 2003, and it was in 2012 that they finally found clear evidence of successful synthesis.**

● to produce the new element は副詞的用法の不定詞。森田氏のチームが実験を始めた目的を表している。

● it is[was] ～ that ... は「…するのは～だ［だった］」と「～」の部分を強調する構文。ここでは in 2012 が強調されている。

🖋**確認** （　　）内に適切な語を入れなさい。
ア．私たちが食べたいのはラーメンだ。
It (　　) ramen (　　) we want to eat.
イ．私たちを助けてくれたのはジェームズだった。
It (　　) James (　　) helped us.

③ **During the nine years, they repeated the experiment about 400 trillion times, and they were able to create their target three times.**
● 400 trillion times は「400兆回」の意味。
● were able to ~は「~することができた」の意味。実際に何かに挑戦してそれができたという場合は、couldではなくwas[were] able to ~を使う。
🖋**確認** （　　）内に適切な語を入れなさい。
ア．彼らは昨日宿題を終えることができた。
They (　　) (　　) to finish their homework yesterday.
イ．彼女は2歳でひらがなを読むことができた。
She (　　) (　　) to read *hiragana* at the age of two.
● their target はニホニウムをさす。

④ **Nihonium is not a stable element and can exist only for two milliseconds.**
● stable は「安定した」の意味。

⑤ **Therefore, it is not considered to provide direct benefits for people's daily lives.**
● it は④のNihoniumをさす。
● provide は「~を与える、提供する」、benefit は「利益」、daily life は「日常生活」の意味。

⑥ **However, exploring elements offers fundamental knowledge about the world itself.**
● exploring elements が文の主語。
● explore は「~を調査する、探求する」の意味。
● fundamental knowledge about the world itself が動詞offersの目的語になっている。

⑦ **This knowledge is essential for scientists to conduct more practical research.**
- ここでの〈形容詞 + for ... to ～〉は「…が［にとって］～するために―だ」の意味。
- conduct は「～を行う」の意味。

⑧ **Morita says, "We named the new element 'nihonium' to thank people in Japan for their support.**
- 〈name + O + C〉で「O を C と名づける」の意味。ここでは O が the new element、C が 'nihonium' である。
- to thank ～は不定詞の副詞的用法。新しい元素をニホニウムと名づけた目的を表している。

⑨ **We hope that they will be proud of Japan and be interested in science when they see nihonium on the periodic table.**
- 文末の on the periodic table までが that 節。
- be proud of ～は「～を誇りに思う」の意味。

⑩ **We will be happy if that leads to the development of science and technology in Japan in the future."**
- 文末の in the future までが if 節。
- that は⑨の that 節の内容をさす。
- lead to ～は「～につながる、結びつく」の意味。

確認問題

1 下線部の発音が同じものには○、違うものには×を（　　）に書き入れなさい。

(1) hydrogen — ultrahigh （　　　）

(2) synthesis — therefore （　　　）

(3) compose — nihonium （　　　）

(4) provide— millisecond （　　　）

(5) target — artificially （　　　）

2 □から最も適切な語を選び、（　　）に書き入れなさい。

(1) The cars were damaged in the (　　　).

(2) There will be no (　　　) impact from the typhoon.

(3) We will learn (　　　) English grammar next week.

(4) They have observed the (　　　) movements of the planets.

(5) Our company's sales will be over three (　　　) yen.

| periodic | direct | collision | fundamental | trillion |

3 日本語に合うように、（　　）内に適切な語を入れなさい。

(1) 彼が有罪である証拠は何もなかった。

There was no (　　　) that he was guilty.

(2) 彼女は仕事を通じて実用的な日本語の知識を得た。

She got (　　　) knowledge of Japanese through her job.

(3) これらのダイヤモンドは人工的に作られた。

These diamonds were (　　　) produced.

(4) したがって、ガソリンの価格が上昇した。

(　　　), the price of gasoline has increased.

(5) この広告のターゲットは10代の若者だ。

The (　　　) for this advertisement is the teenage market.

4 日本語に合うように、（　　）内に適切な語を入れなさい。

(1) その恐竜は福井にちなんでフクイサウルスと名づけられた。

The dinosaur was （　　　） Fukuisaurus （　　　） Fukui.

(2) 被災地はボランティアの人たちの支援に感謝した。

The disaster area （　　　） the volunteers （　　　） their support.

(3) ピンク色はかつて男の子の色だとみなされていた。

Pink was once （　　　） （　　　） be a color for boys.

(4) ウィリアムズ夫妻は子どもたちを誇りに思っている。

Mr. and Mrs. Williams are （　　　） （　　　） their children.

(5) 私はその人気のレストランを予約することができた。

I was （　　　） （　　　） make a reservation at the popular restaurant.

5 次の英語を日本語に訳しなさい。

(1) It was my sister that ate my pudding.

_____

(2) I went to the supermarket to buy some tomatoes.

_____

(3) This is a picture taken at the school festival.

_____

6 日本語に合うように、[　　]内の語句を並べかえなさい。

(1) あれは私たちが試合をした体育館だ。

That is [gym / played / where / the / we] our game.

That is _____ our game.

(2) 私たちは友だちを1時間ずっと待っている。

We [waiting / been / our friend / have / for] for one hour.

We _____ for one hour.

(3) 彼らは犬をムギと名づけた。

[their / they / Mugi / dog / named].

_____ .

7 次の英文を読み、設問に答えなさい。

In 2017, a new element was officially added to the periodic table of elements. It is nihonium (Nh). Nihonium is unique ①( ) it is the first element found outside of Western countries. It was discovered in Japan by a researcher, Morita Kosuke, and his team. ②The element was ( ) ( ) the place where it was found, *Nihon*.

③An element is a basic substance that composes things in the world. Hydrogen (H), oxygen (O), and carbon (C) are examples of such elements. All the elements naturally ④(exist) in this world had been found by the middle of the 20th century. ⑤Since then, scientists have been trying to create a new element artificially.

(1) 空所①に入る最も適切な語を選び、記号で答えなさい。

ア．because　イ．that　ウ．if　エ．when　　　　( )

(2) 下線部②が「その元素は、発見された場所である日本にちなんで名づけられた。」という意味になるように、空所に当てはまる2語の英語を書きなさい。

_____ _____

(3) 下線部③を日本語に訳しなさい。

_____

(4) ④の単語を適切な形に直しなさい。

_____

(5) 下線部⑤を日本語に訳しなさい。

_____

(6) 本文の内容に合うように、次の質問に英語で答えなさい。

When was nihonium added to the periodic table of elements?

_____

8 次の英文を読み、設問に答えなさい。

Nihonium was ①(synthesize) by the collision of two elements, zinc (Zn) and bismuth (Bi), at an ultrahigh speed in a special machine. Morita's team started the experiment to produce the new element in 2003, and it was in 2012 that they finally found clear evidence of successful synthesis. During the nine years, they repeated the experiment about 400 trillion times, and they were able to create their target three times.

Nihonium is not a stable element and can exist only for two milliseconds. ②( ), it is not considered to provide direct benefits for people's daily lives. ③( ), exploring elements offers fundamental knowledge about the world itself. ④This knowledge is [to / scientists / essential / conduct / for] more practical research.

Morita says, "⑤We named the new element 'nihonium' to thank people in Japan for their support. We hope that they will be proud of Japan and be interested in science when they see nihonium on the periodic table. We will be happy if that leads to the development of science and technology in Japan in the future."

(1) ①の単語を適切な形に直しなさい。

_____

(2) 空所②③に入る最も適切な語をそれぞれ選び、記号で答えなさい。

ア. Also　　イ. However　　ウ. Therefore　　エ. First

②(　　)　　③(　　)

(3) 下線部④が「この知識は、科学者がより実用的な研究を行うために必要不可欠だ。」という意味になるように、[　]内の語を並べかえなさい。

This knowledge is _____

_____ more practical research.

(4) 下線部⑤を日本語に訳しなさい。

_____

Tea in Desert Climates

 読解のポイント

教科書 p.64

1. 1人当たりのお茶の消費量が多い国はどのような国ですか。
2. なぜ中東ではお茶の文化が発展したのですか。

Setting **An ALT is talking about tea.**

① What countries do you think of when you hear the word "tea"? You may come up with China, the UK, or Japan. ② It is true that a lot of tea is consumed in these countries. ③ However, when it comes to consumption per capita, some Middle Eastern and African countries such as Turkey, Morocco, Iran, and Egypt are major consumers of tea. ④ For example, in Turkey, people love to drink chai, strong black tea with sugar. ⑤ Similarly, Morocco is famous for its mint tea that consists of Chinese green tea, sugar, and spearmint leaves. Why is tea popular in the Middle East and Africa?

There are various reasons behind its popularity. ⑥ In the case of the Middle East, geography is an important factor. ⑦ The Middle East is located between Asia and Europe. ⑧ Asia is a major tea production area, and Europe is a major tea consumption area. ⑨ Tea culture in the Middle East has developed because of the long history of tea trade between these two areas.

単語・語句の研究

☐ come up with ～	～を思いつく
☐ when it comes to ～	～のこと［話］になると 例 When it comes to photography, he is an expert.（写真のこととなると、彼は専門家だ）
☐ consumption [kənsΛmpʃn]	图 消費
☐ capita [kǽpətə]	图 caput（頭）の複数形
☐ per capita	1人当たりの 例 This figure shows the annual consumption of rice per capita. （この数字は、1人当たりの米の年間消費量を表している）

UNIT 2

☐ **Eastern** [íːstərn]	形 東の、東にある 参考 east（東）
☐ **Morocco** [mərákou]	名 モロッコ（（アフリカ北西部の国））
☐ **Iran** [iráːn]	名 イラン（（アジア南西部の国））
☐ **chai** [tʃái]	名 チャイ
☐ **similarly** [símələrli]	副 同様に
☐ **mint** [mínt]	名 ミント、ハッカ
☐ **spearmint** [spíərmint]	名 オランダハッカ、スペアミント
☐ **popularity** [pàpjəlǽrəti]	名 人気 参考 popular（人気のある）
☐ in the case of ～	～の場合は、～に関しては 例 In the case of Japan, the birth rate has been declining for more than five years. （日本の場合は、出生率が 5 年以上低下し続けている）

 解説

① **What countries do you think of when you hear the word "tea"?**
- think of ～は「～を思いつく、考えつく」の意味。

② **It is true that a lot of tea is consumed in these countries.**
- It は形式主語で、that 節（that ～ these countries）が真の主語。
- consume は「～を消費する」の意味で、ここでは受け身になっている。

③ **However, when it comes to consumption per capita, some Middle Eastern and African countries such as Turkey, Morocco, Iran, and Egypt are major consumers of tea.**
- some Middle Eastern ～ and Egypt がこの文の主語。
- consumption は「消費」、Middle Eastern は「中東の」、consumer は「消費者」の意味。

④ **For example, in Turkey, people love to drink chai, strong black tea with sugar.**
- strongは「(お茶やコーヒーなどが)濃い」、black teaは「紅茶」の意味。
- chaiとstrong black tea with sugarは同格の関係。

⑤ **Similarly, Morocco is famous for its mint tea that consists of Chinese green tea, sugar, and spearmint leaves.**
- be famous for ～は「～で有名である」、consist of ～は「～から成り立つ」の意味。
- that は関係代名詞で、that consists of Chinese green tea, sugar, and spearmint leavesが先行詞its mint teaを後ろから修飾している。

⑥ **In the case of the Middle East, geography is an important factor.**
- geographyは「地理」、factorは「要素、要因」の意味。

⑦ **The Middle East is located between Asia and Europe.**
- be locatedは「位置する、ある」の意味。

⑧ **Asia is a major tea production area, and Europe is a major tea consumption area.**
- productionは「生産」の意味。

⑨ **Tea culture in the Middle East has developed because of the long history of tea trade between these two areas.**
- 〈has＋過去分詞〉は現在完了で、ここでは「(ずっと)～した、～してきた」の意味。
- ✐ 確認 (　　)内に適切な語を入れなさい。
  - ア. 彼女は医師として15年間働いてきた。
    - She (　　) (　　) as a doctor for 15 years.
  - イ. その島では地震が続いている。
    - There (　　) (　　) earthquakes on the island.
- tradeは「貿易」の意味。
- these two areasは前文のAsiaとEuropeをさす。

教科書 p.65

 読解のポイント

1. アフリカではどのようにお茶の文化が根付きましたか。
2. なぜ気候や宗教がお茶の消費に影響を与えるのでしょうか。

① As for Africa, politics cannot be overlooked. ② In the 19th and 20th centuries, Great Britain colonized some countries in Africa such as Kenya and Tanzania. ③ Because Great Britain built large tea plantations in these countries, the custom of drinking tea took root there. ④ Gradually, tea culture expanded to other areas in Africa.

⑤ The natural environment also plays a crucial role. ⑥ In the dry air of the Middle East and Africa, people frequently drink tea to satisfy their thirst. ⑦ Furthermore, many people in these areas believe in Islam, which bans drinking alcohol. ⑧ This rule leads to Muslims' consumption of tea.

⑨ How people enjoy tea is different, depending on the country. ⑩ Yet, one feature is common. ⑪ As we know, tea helps people relax and socialize.

Ⓐ Ⓑ Ⓒ **単語・語句の研究**

☐ as for ～	～について言えば 例 As for sports, I am not good at any of them. （スポーツについては、私はどれも得意ではない）
☐ politics [pálətiks]	名 政治 参考 political（政治の）
☐ **overlook (ed)** [òuvərlúk(t)]	動 ～を見逃す、見落とす
☐ colonize (d) [kálənàiz(d)]	動 ～に植民地をつくる、植民地化する 参考 colony（植民地）
☐ plantation (s) [plæntéiʃn(z)]	名 大農園、栽培場
☐ take root	根付く、定着する 例 Working from home took root in some companies. （一部の企業では在宅勤務が定着した）
☐ **crucial** [krúːʃl]	形 非常に重要な

59

☐ **frequently** [frí:kwəntli]	副 たびたび、頻繁に
	参考 frequent（たびたびの、頻繁な）
☐ **furthermore** [fə́ːrðərmɔ̀ːr]	副 さらに、その上
☐ believe in ～	（宗教）を信仰する
	例 About 30 percent of Korean people believe in Christianity.
	（韓国人の約30%がキリスト教を信仰している）
☐ Islam [islá:m]	名 イスラム教
☐ Muslim [mʌ́zləm]	名 イスラム教徒

 解説

① **As for Africa, politics cannot be overlooked.**
- 〈助動詞 + be + 過去分詞〉の受け身の文。cannot be overlookedはここでは「見逃すことはできない」と能動態で訳すほうが自然。

② **In the 19th and 20th centuries, Great Britain colonized some countries in Africa such as Kenya and Tanzania.**
- Great Britain は「英国、イギリス」、Kenya は「ケニア（アフリカ東部の国）」、Tanzania は「タンザニア（アフリカ中東部の国）」の意味。

③ **Because Great Britain built large tea plantations in these countries, the custom of drinking tea took root there.**
- these countries と there は、②の英国が植民地としていた国々をさす。
- custom は「習慣」の意味。

④ **Gradually, tea culture expanded to other areas in Africa.**
- gradually は「だんだんと、次第に」、expand to ～ は「～へと広がる、拡大する」の意味。

⑤ **The natural environment also plays a crucial role.**
- play a[an] ～ role は「～な役割を果たす」の意味。

⑥ **In the dry air of the Middle East and Africa, people frequently drink tea to satisfy their thirst.**
- dry は「乾燥した」、satisfy は「～を満たす」、thirst は「（のどの）渇き」の意味。

- to satisfy their thirstは不定詞の副詞的用法で、people frequently drink teaの目的を表している。

⑦ **Furthermore, many people in these areas believe in Islam, which bans drinking alcohol.**

- these areasは⑥のthe Middle East and Africaをさす。
- whichは関係代名詞（非制限用法）。〈, which 〜〉で「そしてそれは〜」の意味。「これらの地域の多くの人々はイスラム教を信仰しているが、それ（＝イスラム教）は〜」と先行詞Islamについて説明を加えている。
- 確認　（　　）内に適切な語を入れなさい。
  ア．あなたは法隆寺を見ることができますが、それは世界最古の木造建築です。
  You can see Horyuji Temple, (　　) (　　) the oldest wooden building in the world.
  イ．私はコンピュータを持っていますが、それは中国製です。
  I have a computer, (　　) (　　) made in China.
- banは「〜を禁止する」、alcoholは「アルコール飲料、酒」の意味。

⑧ **This rule leads to Muslims' consumption of tea.**

- This ruleは⑦の酒を飲んではいけないという規則をさす。
- lead to 〜は「〜につながる、結びつく」の意味。

⑨ **How people enjoy tea is different, depending on the country.**

- howを使った間接疑問文。〈how + S + V〉で「Sがどのように〜するか」の意味。How people enjoy teaはこの文の主語になっている。
- 確認　（　　）内に適切な語を入れなさい。
  ア．外国では人々がどのように誕生日を祝うかを知りたい。
  I want to know (　　) (　　) celebrate birthdays in other countries.
  イ．あなたがどのように服を買うのか教えてください。
  Please tell me (　　) (　　) buy your clothes.
- depending on 〜は「〜によって」の意味。

⑩ **Yet, one feature is common.**

● yetは「けれども、しかし」、featureは「特徴、特色」、commonは「共通の」の意味。

⑪ **As we know, tea helps people relax and socialize.**

● 〈help + O + 動詞の原形〉は「Oが〜するのを助ける」の意味。

✎ 確認 　（　　　）内に適切な語を入れなさい。

ア．その肥料は植物が成長するのを助ける。

The fertilizer (　　　) plants (　　　).

イ．彼が祖母へのプレゼントを選ぶのを手伝ってくれますか。

Can you (　　　) (　　　) choose a gift for his grandmother?

● socializeは「社交的に交際する」の意味。

確認問題

1 下線部の発音が同じものには○、違うものには×を（　　）に書き入れなさい。

(1) Moroc<u>c</u>o — <u>o</u>verlook （　　　）

(2) r<u>o</u>le — r<u>oo</u>t （　　　）

(3) f<u>ea</u>ture — sp<u>ea</u>rmint （　　　）

(4) <u>ea</u>stern — <u>E</u>gypt （　　　）

(5) <u>f</u>requently — geogra<u>ph</u>y （　　　）

2 ☐ から最も適切な語を選び、（　　）に書き入れなさい。

(1) （　　　　　） leaves have a fresh smell and taste.

(2) Japan imports large amounts of octopus from （　　　　　）.

(3) Would you like a cup of （　　　　）?

(4) This （　　　　） grows coffee.

(5) People who believe in （　　　） are called Muslims.

plantation	Morocco	Islam	chai	mint

3 日本語に合うように、（　　）内に適切な語を入れなさい。

(1) そのゲームは10年前に人気を集めた。

The game gained （　　　　） 10 years ago.

(2) 彼女は政治に関心がある。

She is interested in （　　　　）.

(3) オリーブオイルはイタリア料理にとって非常に重要な材料だ。

Olive oil is a （　　　　） ingredient in Italian food.

(4) ハイチはフランスに植民地化されていた。

Haiti had been （　　　　） by France.

(5) さらに、彼は生涯ゴールデンスラムを達成した初のテニス選手だ。

（　　　　　）, he is the first tennis player to achieve a Career Golden Slam.

4 日本語に合うように、(　　　)内に適切な語を入れなさい。

(1) 私は店がこの地域に根付くことを願っている。

I hope our store will (　　　) (　　　) in this community.

(2) アメリカの場合、サマータイムは3月に始まる。

In the (　　　) (　　　) the U.S., daylight saving time starts in March.

(3) 色については、黒、白、ネイビーがございます。

(　　　) (　　　) the colors, black, white, and navy are available.

(4) 何かアイディアを思いつきましたか。

Did you (　　　) (　　　) with any ideas?

(5) 卓球のこととなると、だれも彼には敵わない。

When (　　　) (　　　) to table tennis, no one can beat him.

5 次の英語を日本語に訳しなさい。

(1) I have a red bike, which my father gave me.

_____

(2) Please help me move the table.

_____

(3) We have lived in Kanazawa for 10 years.

_____

6 日本語に合うように、[　　　]内の語句を並べかえなさい。

(1) どのように米を料理するかは国によって異なる。

[people / rice / how / cook] differs from country to country.

_____ differs from country to country.

(2) このエレベーターは使用できない。

[be / cannot / this / used / elevator].

_____.

(3) 水は水素と酸素で構成される。

[of / and oxygen / hydrogen / consists / water].

_____.

7 次の英文を読み、設問に答えなさい。

What countries do you think of when you hear the word "tea"? You may come up ①(   ) China, the UK, or Japan. It is true that a lot of tea is consumed in these countries. However, ②(   ) (   ) (   ) to consumption per capita, some Middle Eastern and African countries such as Turkey, Morocco, Iran, and Egypt are major consumers of tea. For example, in Turkey, people love to drink chai, strong black tea with sugar. Similarly, Morocco is famous for its mint tea that consists of Chinese green tea, sugar, and spearmint leaves. Why is tea ③(   ) in the Middle East and Africa?

There are various reasons behind its popularity. ④In the case of the Middle East, geography is an important factor. The Middle East is located between Asia and Europe. Asia is a major tea production area, and Europe is a major tea consumption area. Tea culture in the Middle East has developed because of the long history of tea trade between these two areas.

(1) 空所①に入る最も適切な語を選び、記号で答えなさい。

　　ア. to　　イ. for　　ウ. on　　エ. with　　　　　　　(　　)

(2) 下線部②が「1人当たりの消費量となると」という意味になるように、空所に当てはまる3語の英語を書きなさい。

　　_____　_____　_____

(3) 空所③に入る最も適切な語を選び、記号で答えなさい。

　　ア. strong　　イ. popular　　ウ. sweet　　エ. green　　(　　)

(4) 下線部④を日本語に訳しなさい。

　　_____

(5) 本文の内容に合うように、次の質問に英語で答えなさい。

　　What kind of tea do people in Turkey love to drink?

　　_____

8 次の英文を読み、設問に答えなさい。

As for Africa, politics cannot be ①(overlook). In the 19th and 20th centuries, Great Britain colonized some countries in Africa such as Kenya and Tanzania. Because Great Britain built large tea plantations in these countries, the custom of drinking tea ②(   ) root there. Gradually, tea culture expanded to other areas in Africa.

The natural environment also plays a crucial role. In the dry air of the Middle East and Africa, people frequently drink tea to satisfy their thirst. Furthermore, ③<u>many people in these areas (   ) (   ) Islam</u>, which bans drinking alcohol. This rule leads to Muslims' consumption of tea.

④<u>How people enjoy tea is different, depending on the country.</u> Yet, one feature is common. As we know, ⑤[relax / helps / and / tea / people] socialize.

(1) ①の単語を適切な形に直しなさい。　　　　　　　_____

(2) 空所②に入る最も適切な語を選び、記号で答えなさい。

　　ア. took　　イ. put　　ウ. set　　エ. went　　　　　　（　　　）

(3) 下線部③が「これらの地域の多くの人々はイスラム教を信仰している」という意味になるように、空所に当てはまる2語の英語を書きなさい。

　　_____　_____

(4) 下線部④を日本語に訳しなさい。

(5) 下線部⑤が「お茶は人々がリラックスしたり交流したりするのを助ける」という意味になるように、[　]内の語を並べかえなさい。

　　_____ socialize

(6) 本文の内容に合うように、次の質問に英語で答えなさい。

　　Why do people frequently drink tea in the Middle East and Africa?

_____

LESSON 4

The Benefits of Origami

 読解のポイント

教科書 p.72 *l*.1〜p.72 *l*.12

1. 折り紙を折ると地図が読みやすくなるのはなぜですか。
2. 折り紙を折ると自制心が養われるのはなぜですか。

Setting **A student is giving a presentation about origami.**

(1) Most of you probably have the experience of folding paper, or origami. (2) Today, I'd like to talk about some fascinating aspects of origami. (3) According to a Japanese professor, it has four main positive effects on your brain.

(4) First, origami can improve your ability to recognize space. (5) Making a shape from a square sheet of paper can enhance the skill of connecting 2-D and 3-D objects. (6) This skill may help you find a location from a map.

(7) Second, origami can improve your ability to control your actions based on rules. (8) To complete one origami work, you need to follow the step-by-step instructions. (9) Origami can be a good exercise for promoting your self-control.

A B C 単語・語句の研究

☐ **fascinating** [fǽsinèitiŋ]	形 魅力的な 参考 fascinate (〜を魅了する)
☐ **ability** [əbíləti]	名 能力 参考 able (有能な)
☐ **enhance** [inhǽns]	動 〜を高める
☐ 2-D	形 2次元の、平面的な
☐ 3-D	形 3次元の、立体的な
☐ **object (s)** [ábdʒikt(s)]	名 物、物体
☐ **location** [loukéiʃn]	名 位置、場所
☐ step-by-step	形 一歩一歩の、段階的な
☐ **self-control** [sèlfkəntróul]	名 自制、セルフコントロール

解説

① **Most of you probably have the experience of folding paper, or origami.**
- foldは「(紙や布など)を折りたたむ」の意味で、ここでは動名詞になっている。
- orはここでは「すなわち」という意味で、folding paperをorigamiと言い換えるために使われている。

② **Today, I'd like to talk about some fascinating aspects of origami.**
- aspectは「面、側面」の意味。

③ **According to a Japanese professor, it has four main positive effects on your brain.**
- itは前文のorigamiをさす。
- according to 〜は「〜によると」、professorは「教授」、brainは「脳」の意味。
- このあとの第2〜5段落で、four main positive effectsについて説明される。

④ **First, origami can improve your ability to recognize space.**
- improveは「〜を改善する、向上させる」、recognizeは「〜を認識する」の意味。
- to recognize spaceは不定詞の形容詞的用法で、your abilityを後ろから修飾している。

  🖊️ **確認** (　　) 内に適切な語を入れなさい。
  ア. ここは走るのによい場所だ。
  　　This is a good place (　　　) (　　　).
  イ. 私には本棚を整理する時間が必要だ。
  　　I need (　　　) (　　　) organize my bookshelves.

⑤ **Making a shape from a square sheet of paper can enhance the skill of connecting 2-D and 3-D objects.**
- Making 〜 paperがこの文の主語。
- shapeは「形」、squareは「正方形の、四角の」、skillは「技能、スキル」、connectは「〜をつなぐ、結びつける」の意味。

⑥ **This skill may help you find a location from a map.**
- This skill は前文の the skill of connecting 2-D and 3-D objects をさす。
- 〈help + O + 動詞の原形〉は「Oが〜するのを助ける」の意味。

⑦ **Second, origami can improve your ability to control your actions based on rules.**
- to control 以下は不定詞の形容詞的用法で、your ability を後ろから修飾している。
- based on 〜は「〜に基づいて」の意味。

⑧ **To complete one origami work, you need to follow the step-by-step instructions.**
- To complete one origami work は不定詞の副詞的用法で、you need to 以下の目的を表している。
- ⌨確認 （　）内に適切な語を入れなさい。
  - ア．私たちはカレーを作るために玉ねぎを買う必要がある。
    We need to buy some onions （　　）（　　）curry.
  - イ．弟は本を借りるために図書館に行った。
    My brother went to the library （　　）（　　）some books.
- complete は「〜を完成させる」、follow は「〜に従う」、instruction は「指示」の意味。

⑨ **Origami can be a good exercise for promoting your self-control.**
- can はここでは「〜でありうる」と可能性を表している。
- promote は「〜を促進する」の意味で、ここでは動名詞になっている。

 **読解のポイント**

教科書 p.72 *l*.13〜p.73

1. 折り紙に長時間集中するとどのような能力が向上しますか。
2. 手先が器用な人だけが折り紙をすべきなのでしょうか。

　① Third, origami can improve your ability to accomplish missions with passion and patience. ② Through the experience of focusing on origami for a long time and completing it, this ability will be enhanced. ③ This is also said to correlate with your academic performance. ④ Of course, you cannot simply say that origami will make you smart. ⑤ Nevertheless, the process of hard work and the sense of accomplishment will surely have a positive influence on you.

　⑥ Last but not least, origami can promote your skill of performing detailed work with your hands. ⑦ It is generally believed that being good or clumsy with your hands is an innate ability. ⑧ However, the skill can be developed at any age by training. ⑨ Even if you are not good at complicated work, you will be able to overcome your clumsiness by practicing origami repeatedly.

　As you can see, origami has a lot of benefits. ⑩ Why don't you make origami a habit? ⑪ Your potential may be unlocked while you enjoy creating a variety of shapes from colorful square sheets of paper.

 **単語・語句の研究**

☐ **accomplish** [əkámpliʃ]	動 〜を成し遂げる	
☐ **passion** [pǽʃn]	名 情熱	
☐ **patience** [péiʃns]	名 忍耐、我慢強さ　参考 patient（忍耐強い）	
☐ **correlate** [kɔ́:rəlèit]	動 関連する、関係する	
☐ **correlate with 〜**	〜と相互に関係する	

例 The percentage of entrepreneurs in the population correlates with the GDP growth rate of the country.
（人口に占める起業家の割合は、その国の GDP成長率と相関関係がある）

☐ **academic** [ækədémik]	形 学問の、学校の
☐ **nevertheless** [nèvərðəlés]	副 それにもかかわらず、それでも
☐ **accomplishment** [əkámpliʃmənt]	名 達成、完了
☐ last but not least	最後に述べるが決して軽んじられないこととして、大事なことを1つ言い残したが 例 Last but not least, I would like to express my gratitude to all of you. （最後になりますが、皆様への感謝をお伝えしたいと思います）
☐ **clumsy** [klʌ́mzi]	形 不器用な
☐ **innate** [inéit]	形 生まれつきの
☐ **training** [tréiniŋ]	名 訓練、トレーニング 参考 train（〜を訓練する）
☐ clumsiness [klʌ́mzinəs]	名 不器用さ
☐ **potential** [pəténʃl]	名 潜在能力、可能性
☐ **unlock (ed)** [ʌnlák(t)]	動 〜を開放する 参考 un-（反対の動作を表す接頭辞）、lock（かぎをかける）

 解説

① **Third, origami can improve your ability to accomplish missions with passion and patience.**
- to accomplish 以下は不定詞の形容詞的用法で、your ability を後ろから修飾している。
- mission は「任務、使命」の意味。

② **Through the experience of focusing on origami for a long time and completing it, this ability will be enhanced.**
- 前置詞 of の目的語は2つ。focusing on 〜 time と completing it である。
- this ability は前文の your ability to 〜 patience をさす。
- 〈will be ＋過去分詞〉は〜「〜されるだろう」の意味。

③ **This is also said to correlate with your academic performance.**
- This は②の this ability、①の your ability to ~ patience をさす。
- be said to ~は「~すると言われている」、performance は「成績」の意味。

④ **Of course, you cannot simply say that origami will make you smart.**
- simply は「単に、ただ」、smart は「賢い」の意味。
- 〈make + O + C〉で「O を C にする」の意味。ここでは C が形容詞（smart）になっている。

  📝**確認** （　　）内に適切な語を入れなさい。
  ア．このエクササイズはあなたをより健康にするだろう。
  This exercise will (　　　) (　　　) healthier.
  イ．私はこの部屋をシックにしたい。
  I want to (　　) this (　　) chic.

⑤ **Nevertheless, the process of hard work and the sense of accomplishment will surely have a positive influence on you.**
- the process ~ accomplishment がこの文の主語。
- surely は「確かに、必ず」の意味。

⑥ **Last but not least, origami can promote your skill of performing detailed work with your hands.**
- your skill 以下が動詞 promote の目的語になっている。
- detailed は「精密な」の意味。

⑦ **It is generally believed that being good or clumsy with your hands is an innate ability.**
- It is believed that ~は「~だと信じられている」の意味。
- being good ~ your hands が that 節内の主語。

⑧ **However, the skill can be developed at any age by training.**
- 〈助動詞 + be + 過去分詞〉という受け身の文。can be developed はここでは「発達させることができる」と能動態で訳すほうが自然になる。

⑨ **Even if you are not good at complicated work, you will be able to overcome your clumsiness by practicing origami repeatedly.**

- even if ～は「たとえ～でも」、complicatedは「複雑な」、overcomeは「～を克服する」、repeatedlyは「繰り返して」の意味。
- practicingは動名詞で、practicing origami repeatedlyが前置詞by「～によって」の目的語になっている。

⑩ **Why don't you make origami a habit?**

- Why don't you ～?は「～してはどうですか。」と提案する表現。
- 〈make + O + C〉は「OをCにする」の意味。ここではCが名詞 (a habit) になっている。
- habitは「習慣」の意味。

⑪ **Your potential may be unlocked while you enjoy creating a variety of shapes from colorful square sheets of paper.**

- 〈助動詞 + be + 過去分詞〉という受け身の文。〈may be + 過去分詞〉は「～されるかもしれない」の意味。
- 確認 （　　）内に適切な語を入れなさい。
  ア．そのウミガメの子は食べられてしまうかもしれない。
    The baby sea turtle (　　) be (　　).
  イ．洗濯物が風に飛ばされてしまうかもしれない。
    The laundry (　　) (　　) blown away by the wind.
- whileは接続詞で、〈while + S + V〉で「Sが～している間に」という意味。
- a variety of ～は「いろいろな～」、colorfulは「色彩に富んだ、カラフルな」の意味。

確認問題

1 下線部の発音が同じものには○、違うものには×を（　　）に書き入れなさい。

(1) patience — passion 　　　　（　　　　）

(2) self-control — location 　　（　　　　）

(3) through — nevertheless 　　（　　　　）

(4) training — innate 　　　　　（　　　　）

(5) fold — correlate 　　　　　（　　　　）

2 ☐☐☐ から最も適切な語を選び、（　　）に書き入れなさい。

(1) Mike finally （　　　　） his heart to us.

(2) The map shows the precise （　　　　） of the restaurant.

(3) I don't know his （　　　　） background.

(4) She has great （　　　） in art.

(5) We were able to （　　　） our goal.

| location | unlocked | accomplish | academic | ability |

3 日本語に合うように、（　　）内に適切な語を入れなさい。

(1) 私は手先が不器用だ。

I'm （　　　　） with my hands.

(2) 彼女には優秀な数学者になる可能性がある。

She has the （　　　） to be a brilliant mathematician.

(3) 彼はサッカーがすべてのスポーツの中で最も魅力的だと思っている。

He thinks soccer is the most （　　　） sport of all.

(4) 私は騒音を我慢できなくなってきた。

I'm losing my （　　　） with the noise.

(5) その盲導犬は1年間訓練を受けた。

The guide dog received （　　　） for one year.

4 日本語に合うように、(　) 内に適切な語を入れなさい。

(1) 最高気温とアイスクリームの売り上げには相関関係がある。

Maximum temperatures (　　　) (　　　) ice cream sales.

(2) 最後になりますが、祖母のメアリーを紹介いたします。

Last but (　　　) (　　　), I'd like to introduce my grandmother, Mary.

(3) たとえその話が本当でも、私は信じられない。

(　　　) (　　　) the story is true, I don't believe it.

(4) ジョーンズ先生に聞いてみてはどうですか。

(　　　) (　　　) you ask Mr. Jones?

(5) 奈良の大仏は金色だったと信じられている。

(　　　) is believed (　　　) the Great Buddha of Nara was golden.

5 次の英語を日本語に訳しなさい。

(1) If it rains, the game may be canceled.

_____

(2) He made his brother angry.

_____

(3) She has a lot of things to do today.

_____

6 日本語に合うように、[　] 内の語を並べかえなさい。

(1) その店ではさまざまな文房具が売られている。

The store [of / a / stationery / sells / variety].

The store _____.

(2) 私たちはスキーをするためにニセコに来た。

We [ski / Niseko / to / came / to].

We _____.

(3) この充電式カイロはモバイルバッテリーとして使える。

This rechargeable warmer [be / a / as / can / used] mobile battery.

This rechargeable warmer _____ mobile battery.

7 次の英文を読み、設問に答えなさい。

Most of you probably have the experience of ①(fold) paper, or origami. Today, I'd like to talk about some fascinating aspects of origami. ②(   ) (   ) a Japanese professor, it has four main positive effects on your brain.

First, origami can improve your ability to recognize space. Making a shape from a square sheet of paper can enhance the skill of connecting 2-D and 3-D objects. ③This skill may help you find a location from a map.

Second, origami can improve ④ your ability to control your actions (   ) (   ) rules. ⑤To complete one origami work, you need to follow the step-by-step instructions. Origami can be a good exercise for promoting your self-control.

(1) ①の単語を適切な形に直しなさい。

_____

(2) 下線部②が「日本人の教授によると」という意味になるように、空所に当てはまる2語の英語を書きなさい。

_____ _____

(3) 下線部③がさすものを日本語で具体的に答えなさい。

_____

(4) 下線部④が「ルールに基づいて自分の行動をコントロールする能力」という意味になるように、空所に当てはまる2語の英語を書きなさい。

_____ _____

(5) 下線部⑤を日本語に訳しなさい。

_____

(6) 本文の内容に合うように、次の質問に英語で答えなさい。

How many positive effects does origami have on your brain?

_____

8 次の英文を読み、設問に答えなさい。

Third, origami can improve your ability to accomplish missions with passion and patience. Through the experience of focusing on origami for a long time and completing it, ①this ability will be enhanced. This is also said to correlate with your academic performance. Of course, you cannot simply say that origami will make you smart. ②Nevertheless, the process of hard work and the sense of accomplishment will surely have a positive influence on you.

Last but not least, origami can promote your skill of performing detailed work with your hands. It is generally believed that being good or clumsy with your hands is an innate ability. However, ③the skill can be developed at any age by training. Even if you are not good at complicated work, you will be able to overcome your clumsiness by practicing origami repeatedly.

As you can see, origami has a lot of benefits. ④[make / don't / a habit / why / you / origami]? Your potential may be unlocked while you enjoy creating a variety of shapes from colorful square sheets of paper.

(1) 下線部①③がさすものを、本文からそれぞれ9語で抜き出して書きなさい。

① _____

③ _____

(2) 下線部②を日本語に訳しなさい。

_____

(3) 下線部④が「折り紙を習慣にしてはどうですか。」という意味になるように、[　]内の語句を並べかえなさい。

_____ ?

(4) 本文の内容に合うように、次の質問に英語で答えなさい。

How can people overcome their clumsiness?

_____

The Mysteries of English Spelling

 読解のポイント 教科書 p.78〜p.79 *l*.8

1. 英語の学習者にとって、スペルが難しいのはなぜですか。
2. 英語のスペルが不規則である理由の1つは何ですか。

Setting This is a blog post about English spelling.

(1) Read these sentences aloud: *What is the height of the ceiling? It's eight meters.*

(2) What do the words *height*, *ceiling*, and *eight* have in common? (3) All these words include the letters *ei*, but the letters are pronounced differently. (4) The same spelling is not always pronounced in the same way. (5) Conversely, some words are spelled differently but are pronounced the same, such as *eight* and *ate*. (6) These examples show that English spelling can be a challenge for learners of the language.

(7) There are two main reasons why English spelling is irregular. (8) First, English words come from many different languages, such as Greek, Latin, and French. (9) Most of these languages use the same Roman alphabet, but they had different sounds and different rules of spelling. (10) When their words became part of the English language, their spellings remained as they were. (11) One example is the word from Italian, *spaghetti*. In this word, the sound [g] is spelled *gh*, and the sound [t] is spelled *tt*. (12) Another example is the letter *g*, which is pronounced in different ways. (13) In the word *anger*, which has a Scandinavian origin, the *g* is a "hard *g*." (14) However, in the word *danger*, which has a French origin, the letter *g* is a "soft *g*." English spelling patterns show the history of the language. (15) English is a mixture of many different languages and developed over a period of hundreds of years.

ABC 単語・語句の研究

☐ **mysteries** [místəriz]   图 謎、秘密
   < **mystery**   参考 mysterious（不思議な）

☐ **conversely** [kɑ̀nvə́ːrsli]	副 逆に、反対に 参考 converse（反対（の））	
☐ **learner (s)** [lə́ːrnər(z)]	名 学習者 参考 learn（〜を学ぶ）	
☐ **irregular** [irégjələr]	形 不規則な 参考 ir-（不〜）、regular（規則的な）	
☐ **Greek** [gríːk]	名 ギリシャ語 参考 Greece（ギリシャ）	
☐ **Roman** [róumən]	形 ローマの、ラテン文字の	
☐ **anger** [ǽŋgər]	名 怒り	
☐ **Scandinavian** [skæ̀ndənéiviən]	形 スカンジナビア語の	
☐ **pattern (s)** [pǽtərn(z)]	名 パターン、傾向	

解説

① **Read these sentences aloud:** *What is the height of the ceiling? It's eight meters.*

- read 〜 aloud は「〜を声に出して読む」の意味。
- :（コロン）は後ろに語句や文を置いて、説明や例示をするのに使われる。ここでは、these sentences を具体的に示す2文が続いている。
- height は「高さ」、ceiling は「天井」の意味。

② **What do the words** *height, ceiling,* **and** *eight* **have in common?**

- have 〜 in common は「〜を共通して持つ」の意味。ここでは疑問詞 what を使った疑問文なので、「共通点は何か」という意味。

③ **All these words include the letters** *ei,* **but the letters are pronounced differently.**

- All these words は②の *height, ceiling,* and *eight* をさす。
- include は「〜を含む」、letter は「文字」の意味。
- pronounce は「〜を発音する」という意味で、ここでは受け身の文なので過去分詞になっている。

④ **The same spelling is not always pronounced in the same way.**
- 受け身の否定文。
- spellingは「つづり、スペル」、not alwaysは「必ずしも〜とは限らない」、in the same wayは「同じように」の意味。

⑤ **Conversely, some words are spelled differently but are pronounced the same, such as *eight* and *ate*.**
- spellは「〜をつづる」という意味で、ここでは受け身の文なので過去分詞になっている。

⑥ **These examples show that English spelling can be a challenge for learners of the language.**
- These examplesは①〜⑤をさす。スペルが同じでも発音が違う語（①〜④）と、スペルが違っても同じ発音の語（⑤）があるということ。
- canはここでは「〜でありうる」と可能性を示している。
- challengeは「課題、難問」の意味。

⑦ **There are two main reasons why English spelling is irregular.**
- whyは関係副詞。〈reason why + S + V 〜〉で「Sが〜する理由」という意味になる。
- 𝒜確認 （　）内に適切な語を入れなさい。
  - ア．それらがマイクが日本に来た理由だ。
    - Those are the （　　） （　　） Mike came to Japan.
  - イ．私は電車が遅延している理由を知らない。
    - I don't know the （　　） （　　） the trains are late.

⑧ **First, English words come from many different languages, such as Greek, Latin, and French.**
- Latinは「ラテン語」の意味。

⑨ **Most of these languages use the same Roman alphabet, but they had different sounds and different rules of spelling.**
- these languagesは前文のGreek, Latin, and Frenchをさす。
- Roman alphabetは「ローマ文字、ラテン文字」の意味。

⑩ **When their words became part of the English language, their spellings remained as they were.**

- theirはどちらも前文のthese languagesをさす。
- remain as they areは「そのままである」の意味。

⑪ **One example is the word from Italian, *spaghetti*.**
- Italianは「イタリア語」の意味。
- the word from Italianと*spaghetti*は同格の関係。

⑫ **Another example is the letter *g*, which is pronounced in different ways.**
- whichは関係代名詞（非制限用法）で、「そしてそれは〜」と先行詞the letter *g*を説明している。
- 🖊️**確認** （　　）内に適切な語を入れなさい。
  - ア．あのタワーは東京スカイツリーで、634メートルの高さがある。
    That tower is Tokyo Skytree, (　　　) is 634 meters high.
  - イ．そのアニメ番組は1969年に放送が始まり、現在でも放送されている。
    The animated program, (　　　) began airing in 1969, is still on the air today.

⑬ **In the word *anger*, which has a Scandinavian origin, the *g* is a "hard *g*."**
- whichは関係代名詞（非制限用法）で、「そしてそれは〜」と先行詞the word *anger*を説明している。
- スカンジナビア語は、スウェーデン語やデンマーク語などの北方ゲルマン語のこと。
- originは「起源、由来」の意味。
- hard *g*は、game、gasなど[g]と発音される音のこと。

⑭ **However, in the word *danger*, which has a French origin, the letter *g* is a "soft *g*."**
- whichは関係代名詞（非制限用法）で、「そしてそれは〜」と先行詞the word *danger*を説明している。
- soft *g*は、orange、gymなど[dʒ]と発音される音のこと。

⑮ **English is a mixture of many different languages and developed over a period of hundreds of years.**
- mixtureは「混合、混ざったもの」の意味。
- overは「〜の間、〜にわたって」、periodは「期間」の意味で、over a period of hundreds of yearsは「何百年にもわたって」という意味になる。

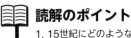 **読解のポイント**

教科書 p.79 *l*.9～p.79 *l*.22

1. 15世紀にどのようなことがありましたか。
2. スペルと同様に、発音も固定されましたか。

① Second, the gap between printing technology and language change created irregular spelling. ② In the 15th century, mass printing of documents became possible. ③ Because of this, the spellings of words became fixed, and they were recognized by people. ④ However, while the spellings remained the same, the pronunciations of some words continued to change over time. ⑤ For example, the word *know* used to be pronounced as [knóu], but the sound [k] gradually became silent. ⑥ Only the spelling was preserved.

⑦ Today, English is still changing. ⑧ Along with the development of social media, we often see a text message that reads "Thanx 4 ur help" instead of "Thanks for your help." ⑨ It is interesting to predict how the spelling or pronunciation of English will change in the future.

A B C 単語・語句の研究

☐ **mass** [mǽs]	形	大量の、大規模な
☐ **document (s)** [dάkjəmənt(s)]	名	文書、書類
☐ **media** [míːdiə] < **medium** [míːdiəm]	名	メディア、媒体
☐ **predict** [pridíkt]	動	～を予測する

 解説

① **Second, the gap between printing technology and language change created irregular spelling.**
- the gap ～ language change がこの文の主語。
- printing は「印刷」の意味。

② **In the 15th century, mass printing of documents became possible.**
- mass printing of documents がこの文の主語。

③ **Because of this, the spellings of words became fixed, and they were recognized by people.**
- fixed は「固定した、一定の」の意味。
- they は the spellings of words をさす。

④ **However, while the spellings remained the same, the pronunciations of some words continued to change over time.**
- while は「〜だけれども」、pronunciation は「発音」、continue to 〜は「〜し続ける」、over time は「時間とともに」の意味。

⑤ **For example, the word *know* used to be pronounced as [knóu], but the sound [k] gradually became silent.**
- used to 〜は「かつては〜だった」の意味。ここでは後ろに受け身の形〈be＋過去分詞〉が続いているので、「かつては〜されていた」となる。
- silent は「発音されない、黙音の」の意味。

⑥ **Only the spelling was preserved.**
- preserve は「〜を保つ、保存する」の意味で、ここでは受け身の文なので過去分詞になっている。

⑦ **Today, English is still changing.**
- today はここでは「今日では、現在では」の意味。

⑧ **Along with the development of social media, we often see a text message that reads "Thanx 4 ur help" instead of "Thanks for your help."**
- along with 〜は「〜とともに、いっしょに」、text message は「メール（スマートフォンや携帯電話でやりとりされる、文字で書かれたメッセージ）」、read は「〜と書いてある」、instead of 〜は「〜の代わりに」、thanks for 〜は「〜をありがとう」の意味。
- that は関係代名詞で、that 以下が先行詞の a text message を後ろから修飾している。
- "Thanx 4 ur help" は "Thanks for your help" を省略して書いたもので、もとの発音を別の文字や数字で表している。スマートフォンや携帯電話では、より少ない文字数で入力できる形が好まれるため。Thanks は ks の部分を

83

xに変えており、forを4 (= four) にしている。yourはyouの部分をuに変えている。

⑨ **It is interesting to predict how the spelling or pronunciation of English will change in the future.**

- It is ... to ～. 「～するのは…だ。」の構文。
- how以下は間接疑問〈how + S + V〉で、「Sがどのように～するか」の意味。動詞predictの目的語になっている。the spelling or pronunciation of Englishが〈how + S + V〉のSである。

✐**確認** ( ) 内に適切な語を入れなさい。

ア. あなたは雪の結晶がどのように作られるか知っていますか。

Do you know ( ) snowflakes are formed?

イ. 私は彼らがどのようにその動画を撮ったのか考えている。

I'm trying to figure out ( ) ( ) took that video.

確認問題

1 下線部の発音が同じものには○、違うものには×を（　　）に書き入れなさい。

(1) m<u>a</u>ss — p<u>a</u>ttern　　　（　　　）

(2) m<u>e</u>dium — m<u>y</u>stery　　　（　　　）

(3) d<u>o</u>cument — R<u>o</u>man　　　（　　　）

(4) irr<u>e</u>gular — pr<u>e</u>dict　　　（　　　）

(5) Scandin<u>a</u>vian — <u>a</u>nger　　　（　　　）

2 ◯◯◯ から最も適切な語を選び、（　　）に書き入れなさい。

(1) This class is for advanced (　　　).

(2) I posted some photos on social (　　　).

(3) We want to reveal the (　　　) of the deep sea.

(4) (　　　) production of cars became possible in the early 20th century.

(5) You have to control your (　　　).

mysteries	mass	learners	anger	media

3 日本語に合うように、（　　）内に適切な語を入れなさい。

(1) schoolという単語はギリシャ語に由来する。

The word *school* comes from (　　　).

(2) 欧米の玄関のドアは内開きだ。反対に、日本の玄関のドアは外開きだ。

Western entrance doors open inward. (　　　), Japanese entrance doors open outward.

(3) その文書の作成者はだれですか。

Who is the author of the (　　　)?

(4) 彼が遅刻するのはいつものパターンだ。

It is the usual (　　　) for him to be late.

(5) 英語には規則動詞と不規則動詞がある。

English has regular and (　　　) verbs.

4 日本語に合うように、（　　）内に適切な語を入れなさい。

(1) リリーとサラには共通点がある。

Lily and Sarah have something (　　　) (　　　　).

(2) 私は母の代わりにそこへ行った。

I went there (　　　) (　　　) my mother.

(3) この文を音読してください。

Please (　　　) this sentence (　　　).

(4) 冥王星はかつて惑星とみなされていた。

Pluto (　　　) (　　　) be considered a planet.

(5) コメントをありがとう。

(　　　) (　　　) your comment.

5 次の英語を日本語に訳しなさい。

(1) Do you know the reason why he is absent?

_____

(2) Kumamoto Castle, which is being restored, can be seen from the garden.

_____

(3) I read an article about how they designed the icon.

_____

6 日本語に合うように、[　　]内の語を並べかえなさい。

(1) 私は高校生になってもサッカーをし続けたい。

I want [soccer / to / play / to / continue] in high school.

I want _____ in high school.

(2) 北村先生は、すべての生徒を同じように扱おうとする。

Ms. Kitamura tries to treat all [in / way / her / the / same / students].

Ms. Kitamura tries to treat all _____.

(3) 外国の文化について学ぶのは楽しい。

[about / to / is / learn / it / fun] foreign cultures.

_____ foreign cultures.

7 次の英文を読み、設問に答えなさい。

①There are two main reasons why English spelling is irregular. First, English words come from many different languages, such as Greek, Latin, and French. Most of these languages use the same Roman alphabet, but they had ②(　　　) sounds and ②(　　　) rules of spelling. When their words became part of the English language, their spellings remained as they were. One example is the word from Italian, *spaghetti*. In this word, the sound [g] is spelled *gh*, and the sound [t] is spelled *tt*. Another example is the letter *g*, which is ③(pronounce) in different ways. In the word *anger*, which has a Scandinavian origin, the *g* is a "hard *g*." However, in the word *danger*, which has a French origin, the letter *g* is a "soft *g*." English spelling patterns show the history of the language. English is a mixture of many different languages and developed over a period of hundreds of years.

(1) 下線部①を日本語に訳しなさい。

(2) 2つの空所②に共通して入る最も適切な語を選び、記号で答えなさい。
　ア．same　　イ．regular　　ウ．French　　エ．different
　　　　　　　　　　　　　　　　　　　　　　　　　（　　　）

(3) ③の単語を適切な形に直しなさい。

(4) 以下の語は、本文中のangerとdangerのどちらの仲間だと考えられるか。記号で答えなさい。
　ア．ginger　　イ．finger
　ⓐ angerの仲間（　　）　　ⓑ dangerの仲間（　　）

(5) 本文の内容に合うように、次の質問に英語で答えなさい。
What language does the word *spaghetti* come from?

8 次の英文を読み、設問に答えなさい。

Second, ①[and / between / language change / the gap / printing technology] created irregular spelling. In the 15th century, mass printing of documents became possible. Because of this, the spellings of words became fixed, and they were recognized by people. However, while the ②(   ) remained the same, the ③(   ) of some words continued to change over time. For example, the word *know* used to be pronounced as [knóu], but the sound [k] gradually became silent. Only the spelling was ④(preserve).

Today, English is still changing. Along with the development of social media, we often see a text message that reads "Thanx 4 ur help" instead of "⑤(   ) (   ) (   ) (   )." ⑥It is interesting to predict how the spelling or pronunciation of English will change in the future.

(1) 下線部①が「印刷技術と言語変化のギャップが不規則なつづりを生み出した」という意味になるように、[　]内の語句を並べかえなさい。

_____ created irregular spelling

(2) 空所②③に入る最も適切な語をそれぞれ選び、記号で答えなさい。

ア. languages　　イ. pronunciations　　ウ. spellings　　エ. meanings

② (　　　　) 　　③ (　　　　)

(3) ④の単語を適切な形に直しなさい。

_____

(4) 空所⑤に適切な4語の英語を書きなさい。

_____ _____ _____ _____

(5) 下線部⑥を日本語に訳しなさい。

_____

(6) 本文の内容に合うように、次の質問に英語で答えなさい。

What became possible in the 15th century?

_____

LESSON 6

A New Discovery in the Nasca Lines

読解のポイント

教科書 p.86〜p.87 *l.*6

1. 坂井正人教授は何を作ろうとしていますか。
2. 研究チームが直面した困難はどのようなものでしたか。

Setting **A research project using AI is introduced in a science magazine.**

① The Nasca Lines are straight lines and figures drawn on the Nasca Pampa in Peru. Many of the figures are geometric patterns and animals such as circles, triangles, hummingbirds, and monkeys. ② The sizes of the Nasca Lines vary from a few meters to over 100 meters. ③ It is thought that some of the oldest drawings were created more than 2,000 years ago. ④ About 1,000 drawings had been found in previous surveys of the area. ⑤ Recently, 580 straight lines and 190 figures were newly discovered.

⑥ These discoveries have been made by a Japanese research team led by Professor Sakai Masato. ⑦ He is an anthropologist studying the Andean Civilization. ⑧ He aims to make a map that overviews all the Nasca Lines. ⑨ Because the civilization had no writing system, he expects to find more about the features of the civilization by making the map. ⑩ He also wants to contribute to the protection of the Nasca Lines from land development.

⑪ At the beginning of the project, the research team faced some difficulties. ⑫ One of them was to obtain high-quality photos of the Nasca Pampa taken from the sky. ⑬ Those photos were necessary to identify new drawings on the vast land. ⑭ The team tried to buy them from a national organization in Peru, but the cost was too high. ⑮ Struggling to find a solution, the team found a generous Japanese company which provided the high-quality photos for free.

ABC 単語・語句の研究

☐ discovery [diskʌ́vəri]　　　　　图 発見
☐ Nasca [nɑ́ːskə]　　　　　　　 形 ナスカ文化の

☐	the Nasca Lines	ナスカの地上絵
☐	pampa [pǽmpə]	名 パンパス((南米の大草原))
☐	the Nasca Pampa	ナスカ台地
☐	geometric [dʒiːəmétrik]	形 幾何学的な　参考 geometry (幾何学)
☐	hummingbird (s) [hʌ́miŋbə̀ːrd(z)]	名 ハチドリ
☐	**previous** [príːviəs]	形 前の、以前の
☐	survey (s) [sə́rvei(z)]	名 調査
☐	**newly** [núːli]	副 新たに
☐	anthropologist [æ̀nθrəpάlədʒəst]	名 人類学者　参考 anthropology (人類学)
☐	Andean [ændíːən]	形 アンデス山脈の　参考 the Andes (アンデス山脈)
☐	**civilization** [sivələzéiʃn]	名 文明
☐	overview (s) [óuvərvjùː(z)]	動 〜を概観する
☐	**identify** [aidéntəfài]	動 〜を確認する、認定する
☐	**vast** [vǽst]	形 広大な

解説

① **The Nasca Lines are straight lines and figures drawn on the Nasca Pampa in Peru.**
- drawn は過去分詞で、drawn 以下が straight lines and figures を後ろから修飾している。
- figure は「図形」の意味。

② **The sizes of the Nasca Lines vary from a few meters to over 100 meters.**
- vary from 〜 to ... は「〜から…までさまざまである」の意味。

③ **It is thought that some of the oldest drawings were created more than 2,000 years ago.**
- It is thought that 〜は「〜だと考えられている」、drawing は「線画」の意味。

④ **About 1,000 drawings had been found in previous surveys of the area.**
- 〈had been + 過去分詞〉は過去完了の受け身の文で、「(過去のある時点で)

〜された」の意味。

確認 （　　）内に適切な語を入れなさい。

ア．その映画は私が生まれる前に作られた。

　　The film (　　) been (　　) before I was born.

イ．彼らがホテルに着いたときには、すでに部屋は掃除されていた。

　　The room (　　) already (　　) cleaned when they arrived at the hotel.

⑤ **Recently, 580 straight lines and 190 figures were newly discovered.**

● 過去の受け身の文。

● discover は「〜を発見する」の意味。

⑥ **These discoveries have been made by a Japanese research team led by Professor Sakai Masato.**

● 〈have been + 過去分詞 + by ...〉は現在完了の受け身の文で、「…によって〜された」の意味。

確認 （　　）内に適切な語を入れなさい。

ア．その恐竜の化石は日本の研究者によって発見された。

　　The dinosaur fossils have (　　) discovered (　　) Japanese researchers.

イ．ある野球選手によって2つのギネス世界記録が達成された。

　　Two Guinness World Records (　　) (　　) set by a baseball player.

● led は lead の過去分詞で、led 以下が a Japanese research team を後ろから修飾している。

⑦ **He is an anthropologist studying the Andean Civilization.**

● studying は現在分詞で、studying 以下が an anthropologist を後ろから修飾している。

⑧ **He aims to make a map that overviews all the Nasca Lines.**

● aim to 〜は「〜することを目指す」の意味。

● that は関係代名詞で、that 以下が先行詞 a map を後ろから修飾している。

⑨ **Because the civilization had no writing system, he expects to find more about the features of the civilization by making the map.**

● the civilization は⑦の the Andean Civilization をさす。

● writing system は「書記体系」の意味。アンデス文明には文字がなかったということ。

- expect to ～は「～するのを期待する」、more は「もっと多くのこと」、feature は「特徴、特色」の意味。
- making は動名詞で、前置詞 by の目的語になっている。

⑩ **He also wants to contribute to the protection of the Nasca Lines from land development.**

- contribute to ～は「～に貢献する」、protection は「保護」、land development は「土地開発」の意味。

⑪ **At the beginning of the project, the research team faced some difficulties.**

- at the beginning of ～は「～の初めに」、face は「～に直面する」の意味。

⑫ **One of them was to obtain high-quality photos of the Nasca Pampa taken from the sky.**

- them は⑪の some difficulties をさす。
- obtain は「～を手に入れる」の意味で、ここでは不定詞の名詞的用法として使われている。
- high-quality は「質の良い、高品質の」の意味。

⑬ **Those photos were necessary to identify new drawings on the vast land.**

- to identify 以下は不定詞の副詞的用法で、Those photos were necessary の目的を表している。
- necessary は「必要な」の意味。

⑭ **The team tried to buy them from a national organization in Peru, but the cost was too high.**

- them は⑫の high-quality photos of the Nasca Pampa taken from the sky をさす。
- national は「国家の、国立の」、organization は「組織、機構」、Peru は「ペルー（（国名））」、cost は「費用」の意味。

⑮ **Struggling to find a solution, the team found a generous Japanese company which provided the high-quality photos for free.**

- struggle to ～は「～しようと奮闘[努力]する」、solution は「解決策」の意味。
- Struggling to find a solution は分詞構文。「解決策を見つけようと奮闘していたときに」の意味。

読解のポイント

1. AIによってどのようなことが解決しましたか。
2. AIを使用したナスカの地上絵の研究で、どのようなことがわかりましたか。

① The next challenge was to identify drawings by closely examining the photos. ② This time-consuming task was done not only by the researchers but also by Japanese student volunteers. ③ Once something like a drawing was found, the research team went to the site and physically checked the drawing. Such a process was slow and labor-intensive.

④ The team wanted to speed up the process and found that AI, or artificial intelligence, could help them examine the photos of the Nasca Pampa. ⑤ If humans examined them, it would take more than ten years. ⑥ However, AI can process them far more quickly. AI learns the parts of the Nasca Lines and looks for possible locations of new drawings. ⑦ Consequently, AI succeeded in detecting a human-like figure that was not spotted by anyone in the team.

⑧ Professor Sakai says, "I didn't think AI was almighty, but it was a big surprise." ⑨ He continues, "Studying the Nasca Lines with AI technology shows us that AI can contribute to a wide variety of research fields, which in turn will help improve our society."

単語・語句の研究

☐ **examin (ing)** [igzǽmən(iŋ)]	動 ～を調査する	
☐ time-consuming [táimkənsù:miŋ]	形 時間のかかる	
☐ **labor-intensive** [léibərinténsiv]	形 大きな労働力を要する	
☐ AI [èiái]	名 人工知能 参考 artificial（人工的な）、intelligence（知能）	
☐ **succeed (ed)** [səksí:d(id)]	動 成功する	
☐ succeed in ～ing	～することに成功する 例 The rocket succeeded in going into space. （そのロケットは宇宙へ行くことに成功した）	

☐ human-like	形 人間のような
☐ almighty [ɔːlmáiti]	形 全能の
☐ in turn	今度は、同様に 例 If you help others, you will be helped by them in turn. （他人を助ければ、今度は自分が他人に助けられるだろう）

 解説

① **The next challenge was to identify drawings by closely examining the photos.**
- to identify は不定詞の名詞的用法で、文の補語になっている。
- closely は「綿密に、念入りに」の意味。
- examining は動名詞で、前置詞 by の目的語になっている。

② **This time-consuming task was done not only by the researchers but also by Japanese student volunteers.**
- 過去の受け身の文。
- task は「仕事、任務」、not only 〜 but also ... は「〜だけでなく…も」の意味。

③ **Once something like a drawing was found, the research team went to the site and physically checked the drawing.**
- once は「〜するやいなや、一度〜すると」の意味。something like a drawing が once 節の主語。
- site は「場所、現場」、physically は「実際に」の意味。

④ **The team wanted to speed up the process and found that AI, or artificial intelligence, could help them examine the photos of the Nasca Pampa.**
- speed up は「〜の速度を増す、〜を加速する」の意味。
- found の主語も The team である。found that 〜は「〜ということを発見した」の意味。
- or は「つまり」の意味で、AI を artificial intelligence と言い換えている。
- could help them の could は時制の一致で過去形になっているだけなので、意味は「〜できた」ではなく「〜できる」だと理解してよい。
- 〈help + O + 動詞の原形〉は「O が〜するのを助ける」の意味。
- them は The team をさす。

⑤ **If humans examined them, it would take more than ten years.**
- 仮定法過去の文。
- them は前文の the photos of the Nasca Pampa をさす。
- take は「(時間など)がかかる」の意味。

⑥ **However, AI can process them far more quickly.**
- them は④の the photos of the Nasca Pampa をさす。
- far は「はるかに、ずっと」と比較級を強調している。

⑦ **Consequently, AI succeeded in detecting a human-like figure that was not spotted by anyone in the team.**
- consequently は「その結果として」の意味。
- detect は「〜を見つける」の意味。ここでは動名詞で、前置詞 in の目的語になっている。
- that は関係代名詞で、that 以下が先行詞 a human-like figure を後ろから修飾している。
- spot は「〜を見つける、発見する」の意味。ここでは受け身なので過去分詞になっている。

⑧ **Professor Sakai says, "I didn't think AI was almighty, but it was a big surprise."**
- AI was almighty の was は時制の一致で過去形になっているだけなので、意味は「〜だった」ではなく「〜である」だと理解してよい。

⑨ **He continues, "Studying the Nasca Lines with AI technology shows us that AI can contribute to a wide variety of research fields, which in turn will help improve our society."**
- Studying 〜 AI technology が坂井教授の発言内の主語。
- a variety of 〜 で「さまざまな〜」、field は「分野、領域」の意味。
- which は関係代名詞(非制限用法)で、AI can 〜 research fields を先行詞として「そしてそのことは〜」と説明している。

🖋 **確認** ( )内に適切な語を入れなさい。

ア．彼女は博士号を取得しており、そのことは私を驚かせた。
She got a PhD, ( ) surprised ( ).

イ．彼は絵が得意であり、そのおかげで彼は有名になった。
He was good at painting, ( ) made ( ) famous.

確認問題

1 下線部の発音が同じものには○、違うものには×を（　　）に書き入れなさい。

(1) c_ivilization — _identify　　（　　　　）

(2) p_ack — N_asca　　（　　　　）

(3) succe_ed — prev_ious　　（　　　　）

(4) _almighty — p_ampa　　（　　　　）

2 ［　　　　］から最も適切な語を選び、（　　）に書き入れなさい。

(1) She removed excess rock to （　　　　） the fossil.

(2) *Shogi* players are using （　　　　） in their research.

(3) （　　　　） have the longest beaks of all birds.

(4) （　　　　） are studying how humans moved from Africa to the rest of the world.

(5) *Kimono* with （　　　　） patterns are recommended for beginners.

AI   geometric   anthropologists   examine   pelicans

3 日本語に合うように、（　　）内に適切な語を入れなさい。

(1) 広大な砂漠の写真が壁にかかっている。

A picture of a （　　　　） desert is on the wall.

(2) 彼らはエラーの原因を特定した。

They （　　　　） the cause of the error.

(3) エジプト文明は紀元前5000年頃に発達し始めた。

Egyptian （　　　　） began to develop around 5000 B.C.

(4) 前回の結果を見てみましょう。

Let's take a look at the （　　　　） result.

(5) これらの紙幣は新しく発行された。

These banknotes were （　　　　） issued.

4 日本語に合うように、( )内に適切な語を入れなさい。

(1) 私たちが森林を守れば、今度は森林が二酸化炭素を吸収し、地球温暖化を防いでくれる。

If we protect forests, they ( ) ( ) will absorb carbon dioxide and prevent global warming.

(2) そのロボットには人間のような指がある。

The robot has ( ) ( ).

(3) 私たちはエベレストに登ることに成功した。

We ( ) ( ) climbing Mt. Everest.

(4) ナスカの地上絵にはたくさんの謎がある。

There are many mysteries about the ( ) ( ).

(5) 彼のレシピは簡単な料理から本格的なものまでさまざまだ。

His recipes ( ) ( ) simple dishes to authentic ones.

5 次の英語を日本語に訳しなさい。

(1) I told the police officer that my bike had been stolen.

_____

(2) He came to the party, which made everyone happy.

_____

(3) AI helps us drive a car.

_____

6 日本語に合うように、[ ]内の語句を並べかえなさい。

(1) それらの問題はエマによって解決された。

Those problems [solved / have / Emma / been / by].

Those problems _____.

(2) そのハーブは肉料理だけでなく魚料理にも使われる。

The herb is used [but / not / meat dishes / only / also / for] for fish dishes.

The herb is used _____ for fish dishes.

(3) 4月の初めに入学式が行われた。

The entrance ceremony was held [of / the / April / beginning / at].

The entrance ceremony was held _____.

7 次の英文を読み、設問に答えなさい。

The Nasca Lines are straight lines and figures ①(draw) on the Nasca Pampa in Peru. Many of the figures are geometric patterns and animals such as circles, triangles, hummingbirds, and monkeys. The sizes of the Nasca Lines vary from a few meters to over 100 meters. ②It is thought that some of the oldest drawings were created more than 2,000 years ago. ③[drawings / about / been / 1,000 / had / found] in previous surveys of the area. Recently, 580 straight lines and 190 figures were newly discovered.

④[have / these / by / made / discoveries / been] a Japanese research team led by Professor Sakai Masato. He is an anthropologist ⑤(study) the Andean Civilization. He aims to make a map that overviews all the Nasca Lines. Because the civilization had no writing system, he expects to find more about the features of the civilization by making the map. He also wants to contribute to the protection of the Nasca Lines from land development.

(1) ①の単語を適切な形に直しなさい。

_____

(2) 下線部②を日本語に訳しなさい。

_____

(3) 下線部③が「以前のこのエリアの調査では、約1,000の線画が見つかっていた。」という意味になるように、[ ]内の語を並べかえなさい。

_____ in previous surveys of the area.

(4) 下線部④が「これらの発見は、日本の研究チームによってなされた」という意味になるように、[ ]内の語を並べかえなさい。

_____ a Japanese research team

(5) ⑤の単語を適切な形に直しなさい。

_____

(6) 本文の内容に合うように、次の質問に英語で答えなさい。
What does Professor Sakai Masato aim to do?

_____

8 次の英文を読み、設問に答えなさい。

The team wanted to speed up the process and found that AI, or artificial intelligence, could help them examine the photos of the Nasca Pampa. If humans examined ①them, it would take more than ten years. However, AI can process them ②(   ) more quickly. AI learns the parts of the Nasca Lines and looks for possible locations of new drawings. Consequently, AI succeeded in ③(detect) a human-like figure that was not spotted by anyone in the team.

Professor Sakai says, "I didn't think AI was almighty, but ④it was a big surprise." He continues, "⑤Studying the Nasca Lines with AI technology shows us that AI can contribute to a wide variety of research fields, which in turn will help improve our society."

(1) 下線部①がさすものを、本文から6語で抜き出して書きなさい。

_____

(2) 空所②に入る最も適切な語を選び、記号で答えなさい。

　ア．many　　イ．so　　ウ．far　　エ．near　　　　（　　　）

(3) ③の単語を適切な形に直しなさい。

_____

(4) 下線部④がさすものを、日本語で具体的に答えなさい。

_____

(5) 下線部⑤を日本語に訳しなさい。

_____

(6) 本文の内容に合うように、次の質問に英語で答えなさい。

　Did Professor Sakai think that AI was almighty?

_____

LESSON 7

Today's Trash is Tomorrow's Treasure

教科書 p.92

 読解のポイント

1. アイサト・シーセイさんが1997年に始めたプロジェクトはどのようなものですか。
2. 路上に捨てられた大量のビニール袋は、どのような問題を引き起こしていましたか。

Setting **Isatou Ceesay is featured in an online article.**

① The concept of upcycling has been receiving attention worldwide. ② Upcycling means using waste to create more valuable products. ③ It is also called "creative recycling." ④ In 1997, a woman in the Gambia, Isatou Ceesay, started a project related to upcycling. ⑤ In her project, Ceesay made colorful purses out of discarded plastic bags with her friends. ⑥ Ever since, the project has contributed to empowering not only Ceesay herself but also many women in the Gambia.

Ceesay was born in a small village in the Gambia in 1972. ⑦ In those days, few children received education there. Ceesay was no exception. ⑧ However, being curious and active, she always questioned what was regarded as "common sense." ⑨ She also wished to solve social problems.

When Ceesay was 25, she met volunteer workers of the US Peace Corps. ⑩ She learned how to recycle waste from them. ⑪ At that time, waste disposal methods had not been established in the Gambia, and a lot of plastic bags were thrown away on the streets. ⑫ Those plastic bags resulted in serious problems such as malaria outbreaks, animal deaths, and poor harvests. ⑬ After learning these facts, Ceesay wanted to reduce the number of discarded plastic bags.

A B C 単語・語句の研究

☐ upcycling [ʌ̀psáiklɪŋ]	名 アップサイクル
☐ Gambia [ɡǽmbiə]	名 ガンビア ((西アフリカの国))
☐ Isatou Ceesay [áisətu: síːsèi]	名 アイサト・シーセイ ((人名))

☐ make ~ out of ...	…で~を作る	
	例 They make sandals out of scrap tires. （彼らは廃タイヤでサンダルを作っている）	
☐ discard (ed) [diskáːrd(id)]	動 ~を捨てる	
☐ **exception** [iksépʃn]	名 例外	
☐ be no exception	例外でない	
	例 Many commercial facilities were closed due to COVID-19 pandemic, and movie theaters were no exception.（コロナ禍で多くの商業施設が休業したが、映画館も例外ではなかった）	
☐ regard (ed) [rigáːrd(id)]	動 ~をみなす	
☐ **corps** [kɔ́ːr]	名 軍団、部隊	
☐ Peace Corps	平和部隊((アメリカのボランティア組織))	
☐ disposal [dispóuzl]	名 処分、処理	参考 dispose（~を処理する）
☐ result in ~	~という結果になる、~に終わる	
	例 Our soccer game resulted in a draw. （私たちのサッカーの試合は引き分けに終わった）	
☐ malaria [məlé(ə)riə]	名 マラリア((病名))	
☐ outbreak (s) [áutbrèik(s)]	名 発生、急増	
☐ **harvest (s)** [háːrvəst(s)]	名 収穫、収穫高	

解説

① The concept of upcycling has been receiving attention worldwide.

- The concept of upcycling がこの文の主語。
- 現在完了進行形〈has been + ~ing〉の文。「（ずっと）~している」の意味。
- ✍確認 （　　）内に適切な語を入れなさい。
  - ア．姉は2時間ずっとテレビゲームをしている。

    My sister (　　) been (　　) a video game for two hours.
  - イ．昨日からずっと雪が降り続いている。

    It (　　) (　　) snowing since yesterday.
- concept は「概念」、attention は「注目」、worldwide は「世界中で」の意味。

② Upcycling means using waste to create more valuable products.

- using waste 以下が動詞 means の目的語になっている。

- to createは不定詞の副詞的用法で、using wasteの目的を表している。
- wasteは「廃棄物、不用品」、valuableは「価値のある、役に立つ」、productは「製品」の意味。

③ It is also called "creative recycling."
- SVOCの受け身の文。Itは前文のUpcyclingをさす。
- creativeは「創造的な」、recyclingは「リサイクル、再利用」の意味。

④ In 1997, a woman in the Gambia, Isatou Ceesay, started a project related to upcycling.
- a woman ～ Isatou Ceesay,がこの文の主語。a woman in the GambiaとIsatou Ceesayは同格の関係。
- relatedは過去分詞で、related to upcyclingがa projectを後ろから修飾している。
- relate ～ to ...は「～を…と関係づける」の意味。

⑤ In her project, Ceesay made colorful purses out of discarded plastic bags with her friends.
- purseは「財布、小銭入れ」、plastic bagは「ビニール袋」の意味。

⑥ Ever since, the project has contributed to empowering not only Ceesay herself but also many women in the Gambia.
- 現在完了〈has + 過去分詞〉の文。「(ずっと)～している」の意味。
- ever sinceは「それ以来(ずっと)」、contribute to ～は「～に貢献する」、not only ～ but also ...は「～だけでなく…も」の意味。
- empowerは「～に能力を与える」の意味で、ここでは動名詞になっている。
- herselfは「彼女自身」の意味で、ここではCeesayを強調している。

⑦ In those days, few children received education there.
- in those daysは「当時」、fewは「ほとんどない、わずかしかない」、educationは「教育」の意味。
- thereは前文のin a small village in the Gambiaをさす。

⑧ However, being curious and active, she always questioned what was regarded as "common sense."
- being curious and activeは分詞構文で、理由を表す。because she was

curious and active と同じ意味。

- curious は「好奇心が強い」、question は「～を疑問に思う、疑う」、common sense は「常識」の意味。

⑨ **She also wished to solve social problems.**

- wish to ～は「～したいと思う」、social は「社会の、社会的な」の意味。

⑩ **She learned how to recycle waste from them.**

- how to recycle waste は〈how + to不定詞〉の形で、「～のしかた、～する方法」の意味。
- them は前文の volunteer workers of the US Peace Corps をさす。

⑪ **At that time, waste disposal methods had not been established in the Gambia, and a lot of plastic bags were thrown away on the streets.**

- at that time は「当時」、method は「方法」の意味。
- 前半は〈had not been + 過去分詞〉で、過去完了の受け身の否定文。「（過去のある時点まで）～されなかった」の意味。
- 後半は過去の受け身の文。throw away は「～を捨てる」の意味で、ここでは過去分詞になっている。

⑫ **Those plastic bags resulted in serious problems such as malaria outbreaks, animal deaths, and poor harvests.**

- Those plastic bags は前文にある、路上に捨てられた大量のビニール袋をさす。
- serious は「重大な、深刻な」、poor は「乏しい、わずかな」の意味。

⑬ **After learning these facts, Ceesay wanted to reduce the number of discarded plastic bags.**

- learning は動名詞で、learning these facts が前置詞After の目的語になっている。
- these facts は⑫の内容全体をさす。
- reduce は「～を減らす」の意味。

読解のポイント

1. シーセイさんたちは、プロジェクトを進める上でどのような困難に直面しましたか。
2. ガンビア政府は2015年に何を行いましたか。

(1) After a while, Ceesay came up with the idea of making purses out of discarded plastic bags and selling them. Ceesay and her friends began the project by picking up plastic bags on the streets. After washing and drying the plastic bags, they cut and spun them into yarn. (2) Using the plastic yarn, they successfully made handy purses.

(3) However, their husbands were not happy with their project. The men said that women should focus on household chores. Despite the opposition, Ceesay and her friends never gave up. (4) They got together at night and kept making purses secretly by candlelight. When they completed enough purses, they brought them to a market in the city. The purses were popular and sold out quickly. (5) Ceesay and her friends were so delighted that they decided to continue their project. (6) Their husbands gradually accepted it, realizing that the wives' income supported their families.

Over time, Ceesay's project involved women in nearby villages. (7) Through the project, the women were able to earn money and open their own bank accounts, which led to their financial independence. Currently, over 2,000 women in 40 communities participate in this project. Thus, Ceesay's wisdom brought about a big change in women's social status. (8) In addition, influenced by her project, the Gambian government banned the use of plastic bags in 2015. The wisdom also changed people's attitudes toward the environment.

単語・語句の研究

☐ spun [spán] (< spin)	動（綿など）を紡いで～にする
☐ yarn [jáːrn]	名 織り物用糸、紡ぎ糸
☐ chore (s) [tʃɔ́ːr(z)]	名 雑用、家事

☐ **despite** [dispáit] 　　　　 前 〜にもかかわらず

☐ **opposition** [ùpəzíʃn] 　　 名 反対、妨害　 参考 opposite（反対の、敵対する）

☐ **secretly** [síːkrətli] 　　　 副 秘密に、内緒で

☐ **candlelight** [kǽndllàit] 　 名 ろうそくの明かり

☐ sell 〜 out 　　　　　　　 （商品を）売りつくす
　　　　　　　　　　　　　　 例 All the tickets are sold out.
　　　　　　　　　　　　　　 （チケットは完売した）

☐ **delight (ed)** [diláit(id)] 　 動 〜を大喜びさせる、楽しませる

☐ **account (s)** [əkáunt(s)] 　 名 預金口座

☐ **independence** 　　　　　 名 自立、独立
　 [indəpéndəns] 　　　　　　 参考 independent（自立した）

☐ **wisdom** [wízdəm] 　　　　 名 知恵

☐ bring about 〜 　　　　　 〜をもたらす、引き起こす
　　　　　　　　　　　　　　 例 Heavy rain brought about serious damage in
　　　　　　　　　　　　　　 this area.
　　　　　　　　　　　　　　 （この地域では、大雨が甚大な被害をもたらした）

☐ **status** [stéitəs] 　　　　　 名 地位、身分

☐ Gambian [gǽmbiən] 　　　 形 ガンビアの

 解説

① **After a while, Ceesay came up with the idea of making purses out of discarded plastic bags and selling them.**
- after a while は「しばらくして」、come up with 〜は「〜を思いつく」の意味。
- them は purses をさす。

② **Using the plastic yarn, they successfully made handy purses.**
- Using the plastic yarn は分詞構文で、「〜して」の意味。They used the plastic yarn, and they successfully 〜と同じ。
- successfully は「うまく、成功のうちに」、handy は「便利な、手ごろな」の意味。

③ **However, their husbands were not happy with their project.**
- their はシーセイさんやシーセイさんの友人たちをさす。
- husband は「夫」の意味。

④ **They got together at night and kept making purses secretly by candlelight.**

- They は前文の Ceesay and her friends をさす。
- get together は「集まる、集合する」、keep ～ing は「～し続ける」の意味。
- by はここでは「～で、～によって」の意味で、手段を表す。

⑤ **Ceesay and her friends were so delighted that they decided to continue their project.**

- so ～ that ... は「とても～なので…」、decide to ～は「～することにする」、continue は「～を続ける」の意味。

⑥ **Their husbands gradually accepted it, realizing that the wives' income supported their families.**

- gradually は「次第に、だんだんと」、accept は「～を受け入れる」、realize that ～は「～ということを理解する」、income は「収入」の意味。
- wives は wife「妻」の複数形。
- realizing that ～は分詞構文で、「～したので」の意味。because they realized that ～と同じ。

  確認 ( ) 内に適切な語を入れなさい。

  ア．熱があったので、私は医者に診てもらった。

  ( ) a fever, I went to see a doctor.

  イ．何と言ったらよいかわからなかったので、彼は黙っていた。

  He kept quiet, not ( ) what to say.

⑦ **Through the project, the women were able to earn money and open their own bank accounts, which led to their financial independence.**

- earn は「～を得る、稼ぐ」、lead to ～は「～につながる」の意味。
- which は関係代名詞（非制限用法）で、「そしてそのことは～」と the women ～ bank accounts について説明している。

⑧ **In addition, influenced by her project, the Gambian government banned the use of plastic bags in 2015.**

- in addition は「その上、さらに」、ban は「～を禁止する」の意味。
- influence は「～に影響を及ぼす」の意味で、ここでは過去分詞になっている。influenced by her project は「彼女のプロジェクトに影響を受けて」という意味の分詞構文で、influenced の前に being が省略されている。

確認問題

1 下線部の発音が同じものには○、違うものには×を（　　）に書き入れなさい。

(1) ch<u>o</u>re — c<u>or</u>ps　　　（　　　　）

(2) sp<u>u</u>n — <u>u</u>pcycling　　（　　　　）

(3) candlel<u>igh</u>t — malar<u>i</u>a　　（　　　　）

(4) G<u>a</u>mbia — st<u>a</u>tus　　（　　　　）

(5) y<u>ar</u>n — disc<u>ar</u>d　　（　　　　）

2 ◻◻◻ から最も適切な語を選び、（　　）に書き入れなさい。

(1) We had a good (　　　　) of rice this fall.

(2) I'd like to open a bank (　　　　).

(3) (　　　　) studying hard, she failed the exam.

(4) He was (　　　　) listening to their conversation.

(5) The price of eggs increased due to the (　　　　) of bird flu.

| despite | harvest | secretly | outbreak | account |

3 日本語に合うように、（　　）内に適切な語を入れなさい。

(1) 私たちはその計画への反対を表明した。

We expressed (　　　　) to the plan.

(2) 希望通りの生活を送るためには、経済的自立が必要だ。

Financial (　　　　) is necessary to live the life you want.

(3) 経験は知恵の母ということわざがある。

There is a proverb that says experience is the mother of (　　　　).

(4) 私は古いマンガ本を処分するつもりだ。

I am going to (　　　　) my old comic books.

(5) 彼女は他人の社会的地位を気にしない。

She doesn't care about the social (　　　　) of others.

4 日本語に合うように、(　　) 内に適切な語を入れなさい。

(1) シュークリームは売り切れだ。

The cream puffs are (　　　) (　　　).

(2) 世界中で洪水が頻繁に発生しており、日本も例外ではない。

Floods frequently occur around the world, and Japan is (　　　) (　　　).

(3) 私は古いシャツでブックカバーを作った。

I made a book cover (　　　) (　　　) an old shirt.

(4) AIは新たな産業革命をもたらすだろうか。

Will AI (　　　) (　　　) a new industrial revolution?

(5) その実験は失敗に終わった。

The experiment (　　　) (　　　) failure.

5 次の英語を日本語に訳しなさい。

(1) I can help you, having nothing to do now.

_____

(2) My brother has been cleaning his room for an hour.

_____

(3) This road had not been repaired until last year.

_____

6 日本語に合うように、[　　] 内の語を並べかえなさい。

(1) 私はこの単語の発音のしかたを知りたい。

I want to know [pronounce / how / this / to / word].

I want to know _____.

(2) 彼はとてもわくわくしていたので眠れなかった。

He was [couldn't / excited / so / he / sleep / that].

He was _____.

(3) 私たちは授業に集中しなければならない。

We [on / must / class / focus / the].

We _____.

7 次の英文を読み、設問に答えなさい。

Ceesay was born in a small village in the Gambia in 1972. ①(   ), few children received education there. Ceesay was no exception. However, ② being curious and active, she always questioned what was regarded as "common sense." She also wished to solve social problems.

When Ceesay was 25, she met volunteer workers of the US Peace Corps. She learned ③(   ) (   ) (   ) waste from them. At that time, ④ waste disposal methods [been / in / not / established / had] the Gambia, and a lot of plastic bags were ⑤(throw) away on the streets. Those plastic bags resulted in serious problems such as malaria outbreaks, animal deaths, and poor harvests. After learning these facts, Ceesay wanted to reduce the number of discarded plastic bags.

(1) 空所①に入る最も適切な語句を選び、記号で答えなさい。

ア．In those days　　イ．Now and then　　ウ．One after another

エ．In that case　　　　　　　　　　　　　　（　　　）

(2) 下線部②を以下のように書きかえるとき、空所に適切な語を書きなさい。

_____ _____ _____ curious and active

(3) 下線部③が「廃棄物をリサイクルする方法」という意味になるように、空所に当てはまる3語の英語を書きなさい。

_____ _____ _____

(4) 下線部④が「ガンビアでは廃棄物の処分方法が定められていなかった」という意味になるように、[ ]内の語を並べかえなさい。

waste disposal methods _____ the Gambia

(5) ⑤の単語を適切な形に直しなさい。

_____

(6) 本文の内容に合うように、次の質問に英語で答えなさい。

Did Ceesay receive education when she was a child?

_____

8 次の英文を読み、設問に答えなさい。

However, their husbands were not happy with their project. The men said that women should focus on household chores. ①(　　　) the opposition, Ceesay and her friends never gave up. They got together at night and kept making purses secretly by candlelight. When they completed enough purses, they brought them to a market in the city. ② The purses were popular and (　　　) (　　　) quickly. Ceesay and her friends were so delighted that they decided to continue their project. Their husbands gradually accepted it, ③(realize) that the wives' income supported their families.

Over time, Ceesay's project involved women in nearby villages. Through the project, ④ the women were able to earn money and open their own bank accounts, which led to their financial independence. Currently, over 2,000 women in 40 communities participate in this project. Thus, Ceesay's wisdom brought about a big change in women's social status. In addition, influenced by her project, the Gambian government banned the use of plastic bags in 2015. The wisdom also changed people's attitudes toward the environment.

(1) 空所①に入る最も適切な語を選び、記号で答えなさい。
　　ア. Between　　イ. Without　　ウ. Except　　エ. Despite　　(　　)

(2) 下線部②が「その財布は人気があり、すぐに売り切れた。」という意味になるように、空所に当てはまる2語の英語を書きなさい。
　　_____　_____

(3) ③の単語を適切な形に直しなさい。
　　_____

(4) 下線部④を日本語に訳しなさい。
　　_____

(5) 本文の内容に合うように、次の質問に英語で答えなさい。
　　What did the Gambian government do in 2015?
　　_____

Lesson 8-10
Reading ①, ②

Nap Time at School

読解のポイント

1. 台湾の会社や学校にはどのような習慣がありますか。
2. その習慣にはどのような効果があると言われていますか。

Setting **Students are discussing the Taiwanese custom of taking an afternoon nap.**

Meifen: ① When I came to Japan from Taiwan, I was impressed that schools resumed classes right after the lunch break. ② In fact, it is customary to take an afternoon nap in Taiwan. ③ This custom is practiced even in companies and schools. ④ In my high school in Taiwan, we have a 30-minute break between lunch and afternoon classes. ⑤ During this period, everyone is encouraged to take a short nap. ⑥ Even if you don't feel sleepy, at least you have to lay your head on the desk and try to relax.

⑦ The custom is based on oriental medicine. ⑧ It is believed that sleeping twice a day is essential for your health. ⑨ It is also said that a short nap after lunch leads to high productivity for the rest of the day. ⑩ However, some people believe that schools should not force students to take a nap.

What do you think about having a nap time at school? Do you think Japanese schools should adopt this system?

単語・語句の研究

☐ Taiwan [tàiwáːn]	图 台湾 ((地名))
☐ resume (d) [rizúːm(d)]	動 ～を再開する
☐ customary [kʌ́stəmèri]	形 習慣的な、通例の **参考** custom (習慣)
☐ oriental [ɔ̀ːriéntl]	形 東洋の
☐ oriental medicine	東洋医学
☐ productivity [pròudʌktívəti]	图 生産性 **参考** produce (～を生産する)、productive (生産的な)

UNIT 3

解説

① **When I came to Japan from Taiwan, I was impressed that schools resumed classes right after the lunch break.**
- be impressed that ～は「～ということに感動する、感心する」、right afterは「～のすぐあとで」、breakは「休憩」の意味。

② **In fact, it is customary to take an afternoon nap in Taiwan.**
- itは形式主語で、to take an afternoon napが真主語。
- in factは「実は」、take a napは「昼寝をする」の意味。

③ **This custom is practiced even in companies or schools.**
- 受け身の文。practiceは「(習慣的に) ～を行う、～を実践する」の意味で、ここでは過去分詞になっている。

④ **In my high school in Taiwan, we have a 30-minute break between lunch and afternoon classes.**
- 30-minuteは「30分間の」、between ～ and ... は「～と…の間に」の意味。

⑤ **During this period, everyone is encouraged to take a short nap.**
- 受け身の文。〈encourage + O + to +動詞の原形〉は「Oが～するように促す」の意味で、ここではO = everyoneになっている。
- 確認 ( )内に適切な語を入れなさい。
  ア．先生が私にピアノを習うよう勧めてくれた。
    My teacher encouraged ( ) ( ) learn the piano.
  イ．彼らは休憩を取るよう促された。
    They were ( ) ( ) take a break.

⑥ **Even if you don't feel sleepy, at least you have to lay your head on the desk and try to relax.**
- even if ～は「たとえ～でも」、at leastは「せめて、ともかく」、layは「～を横たえる、置く」の意味。

114

⑦ **The custom is based on oriental medicine.**
- be based on 〜は「〜に基づいている」の意味。

⑧ **It is believed that sleeping twice a day is essential for your health.**
- twice a day は「1日に2回」の意味。
- It is believed that 〜は「〜ということが信じられている」の意味。believe が受け身で使われている。

⑨ **It is also said that a short nap after lunch leads to high productivity for the rest of the day.**
- it is said that 〜は「〜だと言われている」、the rest of 〜は「〜の残り」の意味。
- a short nap after lunch が that 節内の主語。

⑩ **However, some people believe that schools should not force students to take a nap.**
- that は接続詞で、believe that 〜は「〜ということを信じる」の意味。
- 〈force + O + to + 動詞の原形〉は「Oに〜することを強制する」の意味。

読解のポイント

教科書 p.101

1. Ken は昼寝の時間を導入することに賛成ですか。
2. Aya は何をして時間を過ごすことが自分にとっては大切だと言っていますか。

Ken: ① I'm for that system because I often fall asleep in afternoon classes. ② According to a book I read before, we tend to feel sleepy about eight hours after waking up. ③ Therefore, the book recommends that we should take a nap before feeling sleepy. ④ Hearing about the Taiwanese custom, I'm convinced that students should take a nap after lunch. ⑤ If this system were introduced, I wouldn't become sleepy any longer and could focus more on afternoon classes.

Aya: ⑥ Well, I understand what you are saying, Ken. ⑦ But I don't think we need an afternoon nap in our school. ⑧ This is because I'd prefer spending the nap time on something else. ⑨ In particular, since we're graduating soon, I'd like to chat with my friends. ⑩ Personally, spending time with friends is more important than sleeping.

ABC 単語・語句の研究

☐ fall asleep	寝入る、眠りに落ちる 例 I sometimes fall asleep during class. （私はときどき授業中に眠ってしまう）
☐ Taiwanese [tàiwəníːz]	形 台湾の
☐ be convinced that ~	～ということを確信している 例 He is convinced that she will pass the exam. （彼は彼女が試験に合格すると確信している）
☐ chat [tʃǽt]	動 おしゃべりをする
☐ personally [pə́ːrsənəli]	副 個人的には、私自身は 参考 personal（個人的な）

解説

① **I'm for that system because I often fall asleep in afternoon classes.**
- Kenが自分の意見を述べている文。Kenは昼寝の時間を導入することに賛成している。
- forは「〜に賛成して」の意味。

② **According to a book I read before, we tend to feel sleepy about eight hours after waking up.**
- a book I read beforeは接触節で、I read beforeが先行詞a bookを後ろから修飾している。このreadは過去形。
- tend to 〜は「〜する傾向がある」の意味。

③ **Therefore, the book recommends that we should take a nap before feeling sleepy.**
- recommendは「〜を推奨する、勧める」の意味。
- thatは接続詞。

④ **Hearing about the Taiwanese custom, I'm convinced that students should take a nap after lunch.**
- Hearing about the Taiwanese customは分詞構文で、「〜して、そして…」の意味。I hear about the Taiwanese custom, and I'm convinced 〜と同じ。

⏎確認　（　　）内に適切な語を入れなさい。
   ア．その飛行機は午前11時に沖縄を出発し、午後1時に大阪に到着する。
   The plane leaves Okinawa at 11:00 a.m., (　　　　) in Osaka at 1:00 p.m.
   イ．私は6時に起きて、6時30分に朝食を食べる。
   (　　　) (　　　) at 6:00, I have breakfast at 6:30.

⑤ **If this system were introduced, I wouldn't become sleepy any longer and could focus more on afternoon classes.**
- 仮定法過去の文。〈If + S + 動詞の過去形 〜, S' + would + 動詞の原形 ...〉で「もしSが〜なら、S'は…するだろう」の意味。Kenは可能性の乏しい想像について話しているので、仮定法が使われている。

✎**確認** （　　）内に適切な語を入れなさい。

ア．私の髪がもっと長かったら、この髪型に挑戦するのに。

If I (　　　) longer hair, I (　　　) try this hairstyle.

イ．私の部屋がもっと広かったら、私はこのテーブルを買うのに。

If my room (　　) larger, I (　　) buy this table.

● not ~ any longerは「もはや~ない」、focus on ~は「~に集中する」の意味。

⑥ Well, I understand what you are saying, Ken.

● what you are sayingのwhatは関係代名詞であると解釈できる。〈what + S + V ~〉で「SがVすること」の意味。ここでは動詞understandの目的語になっている。

⑦ But I don't think we need an afternoon nap in our school.

● Ayaが自分の意見を述べている文。Ayaは昼寝の時間を導入することに反対している。

● don't think ~は「~でないと思う」の意味。

● thinkのあとに接続詞のthatが省略されている。

⑧ This is because I'd prefer spending the nap time on something else.

● I'd prefer ~ingは「どちらかといえば私は~したい」、spend ~ on ... は「~を…に費やす」、something elseは「何かほかのこと」の意味。

⑨ In particular, since we're graduating soon, I'd like to chat with my friends.

● in particularは「特に」、sinceは「~だから」の意味。

● we're graduating soonは現在進行形で、ここでは確定的な未来を表すために使われている。

⑩ Personally, spending time with friends is more important than sleeping.

● spending time with friendsがこの文の主語。

読解のポイント

1. Harukiは昼寝の時間は何に役立つと言っていますか。
2. Maiは机で寝るとどのようなことが起こると言っていますか。

UNIT 3

Haruki: ① In my opinion, setting a nap time at school is worth a try. ② It would be helpful to make up for my lack of sleep and improve my concentration. University entrance exams are just around the corner. Although I study a lot, I often feel it doesn't bear fruit. ③ That makes me feel more pressure, and I end up staying up late. ④ As a result, I feel sleepy the following day and can't concentrate well. It's a vicious circle. ⑤ I think a nap would make the situation better.

Mai: ⑥ I understand the benefit of taking a nap after lunch. ⑦ However, to be honest, I don't want to take a nap, laying my head on the desk. ⑧ That would definitely cause a stiff neck or stiff shoulders. ⑨ I'm afraid it might have a negative effect on my health. ⑩ If this system were introduced, I'd like to sleep on a bed. But it's not realistic, right? ⑪ In a nutshell, I'm against the system.

A B C 単語・語句の研究

☐ be worth a try	やってみる価値がある 例 I think skydiving is worth a try. （私は、スカイダイビングはやってみる価値があると思う）
☐ make up for ～	～の埋め合わせをする、～を補う 例 They made up for my weak points. （彼らは私の弱点を補ってくれた）
☐ lack [lǽk]	名 不足
☐ lack of ～	～の不足
☐ just around the corner	（時間的に）すぐそこに、間近に 例 Christmas is just around the corner. （もうすぐクリスマスだ）

☐	bear fruit	実を結ぶ、よい結果を生む
☐	**vicious** [víʃəs]	形 悪い
☐	a vicious circle	悪循環
☐	**definitely** [défənətli]	副 確実に
☐	**stiff** [stif]	形 （筋肉などが）こった
☐	a stiff neck	首のこり
☐	stiff shoulders	肩こり
☐	**realistic** [rìːəlístik]	形 現実的な　参考 real（現実の）
☐	nutshell [nʌtʃèl]	名 ごく小さいもの、（木の実の）殻
☐	in a nutshell	要するに、つまり　例 In a nutshell, the plan has failed.（要するに、その計画は失敗した）

解説

① **In my opinion, setting a nap time at school is worth a try.**
- Haruki が自分の意見を述べている文。Haruki は昼寝の時間を導入することに賛成している。
- setting a nap time at school が文の主語。

② **It would be helpful to make up for my lack of sleep and improve my concentration.**
- It は①の setting a nap time at school をさす。
- to make up for ～は不定詞の副詞的用法で、「～するために」の意味。

③ **That makes me feel more pressure, and I end up staying up late.**
- That は前文全体の内容をさす。
- 〈make + O + 原形不定詞〉は「Oに～させる」の意味。ここでは〈make + O + feel ～〉なので、「Oに～を感じさせる」の意味。
- 確認　（　）内に適切な語を入れなさい。
  - ア．私たちのコーチは、私たちにその曲を何度も歌わせた。
    Our coach (　　　) (　　　) sing the song over and over.
  - イ．彼らはメリッサに仕事を手伝わせた。
    They (　　　) Melissa (　　　) with the work.
- pressure は「プレッシャー、困難」、end up ～ing は「結局～することに

120

なる」、stay up late は「夜更かしする」の意味。

④ **As a result, I feel sleepy the following day and can't concentrate well.**
- as a result は「その結果（として）」、the following day は「翌日に」、concentrate は「集中する」の意味。

⑤ **I think a nap would make the situation better.**
- think のあとに接続詞の that が省略されている。
- 〈make + O + C〉は「OをCにする」の意味。

⑥ **I understand the benefit of taking a nap after lunch.**
- benefit は「利益、利点」の意味。

⑦ **However, to be honest, I don't want to take a nap, laying my head on the desk.**
- to be honest は「正直に言って」の意味。
- laying my head on the desk は「～しながら、～して」と付帯状況を表す分詞構文。

⑧ **That would definitely cause a stiff neck or stiff shoulders.**
- That は⑦の to take a nap, laying my head on the desk をさす。
- cause は「～の原因となる、～を引き起こす」の意味。

⑨ **I'm afraid it might have a negative effect on my health.**
- be afraid (that) ～は「～ではないかと心配である」、negative effect は「悪影響」の意味。
- it は⑧全体の内容をさす。

⑩ **If this system were introduced, I'd like to sleep on a bed.**
- 仮定法過去の文。if 節は受け身になっている。
- this system は昼寝の時間のこと。

⑪ **In a nutshell, I'm against the system.**
- Mai が自分の意見を述べている文。Mai は昼寝の時間を導入することに反対している。

読解のポイント

1. Ippeiは昼寝の時間を導入することに賛成していますか。
2. Ippeiは何が最も大切なポイントだと言っていますか。

Ippei: ① I disagree with the system because Aya's and Mai's opinions are persuasive. ② The most important point is whether we have options. If you want to take a nap, you can go ahead with it. ③ If you don't, you can do whatever you like as long as you don't disturb people who are sleeping. ④ This sort of flexibility is crucial. ⑤ I believe each student's free will should be respected. ⑥ For this reason, I'm opposed to the introduction of the system if all students are required to sleep during that time.

Meifen: ⑦ Thank you very much for such a heated discussion. ⑧ It was nice to hear your opinions. ⑨ I'd love to continue exchanging our thoughts on Japanese and Taiwanese customs and cultures.

単語・語句の研究

☐ **option (s)** [ápʃn(z)]	图 選択権、選択の自由
☐ go ahead	進める 例 Please go ahead with the procedure. （手続きを進めてください）
☐ **disturb** [distə́ːrb]	動 〜の邪魔をする
☐ **opposed** [əpóuzd]	形 反対の、対立する
☐ be opposed to 〜	〜に反対である 例 They were opposed to the bill. （彼らはその法案に反対した）
☐ **introduction** [intrədʌ́kʃn]	图 導入 参考 introduce（〜を導入する）
☐ **require (d)** [rikwáiər(d)]	動 〜を必要とする
☐ **heated** [híːtid]	形 白熱した、興奮した

解説

① **I disagree with the system because Aya's and Mai's opinions are persuasive.**
- Ippeiが自分の意見を述べている文。Ippeiは昼寝の時間を導入することに反対している。
- disagree with ～は「～に反対する」、opinionは「意見」、persuasiveは「説得力のある」の意味。

② **The most important point is whether we have options.**
- 〈whether + S + V〉は「SがVするかどうか」の意味。
- **確認** （　）内に適切な語を入れなさい。
  - ア．私はその大学を受験すべきかどうかわからない。
    I don't know (　　　) I (　　　) apply to the university.
  - イ．弟は、母が家にいるかどうか私にたずねた。
    My brother asked me (　　　) Mother (　　　) at home.

③ **If you don't, you can do whatever you like as long as you don't disturb people who are sleeping.**
- If you don'tのあとにwant to take a napが省略されている。
- 〈whatever + S + V〉は「SがVすることは何でも」、as long as ～は「～さえすれば」の意味。
- **確認** （　）内に適切な語を入れなさい。
  - ア．あなたが好きなものを何でも食べていいですよ。
    You can eat (　　　) (　　　) like.
  - イ．両親は、私がしたいことを何でもさせてくれた。
    My parents let me do (　　　) (　　　) wanted.
- whoは関係代名詞で、who are sleepingが先行詞peopleを後ろから修飾している。

④ **This sort of flexibility is crucial.**
- this sort of ～は「こういう～、この種類の～」、flexibilityは「柔軟性、融通性」の意味。

UNIT 3

⑤ **I believe each student's free will should be respected.**

- believe のあとに接続詞の that が省略されている。
- free will は「自由意志」の意味。自由意志とは、強制や支配を受けずに行動を自発的に決定する意志のこと。
- 〈should be + 過去分詞〉は「〜されるべきだ」の意味。
- respect は「〜を尊重する」の意味。ここでは受け身の文なので過去分詞になっている。

⑥ **For this reason, I'm opposed to the introduction of the system if all students are required to sleep during that time.**

- for this reason は「このような理由で、こういうわけで」の意味。
- if all students 〜は「もしすべての生徒が〜ならば」と、Ippei が昼寝の時間を導入することに反対する条件を表している。
- 〈require + O + to + 動詞の原形〉は「O に〜することを要求する」の意味。ここでは be required to 〜と受け身になっているので、「〜することを要求される」の意味。

⑦ **Thank you very much for such a heated discussion.**

- discussion は「議論」の意味。

⑧ **It was nice to hear your opinions.**

- It は形式主語で、to hear your opinions が真主語。

⑨ **I'd love to continue exchanging our thoughts on Japanese and Taiwanese customs and cultures.**

- continue 〜ing は「〜し続ける」、thought は「意見、考え」、on は「〜について」の意味。

確認問題

1 下線部の発音が同じものには○、違うものには×を（　　）に書き入れなさい。

(1) n<u>u</u>tshell — c<u>u</u>stomary　　（　　　　）

(2) v<u>i</u>cious — r<u>e</u>sume　　（　　　　）

(3) opp<u>o</u>sed — <u>o</u>ption　　（　　　　）

(4) l<u>a</u>ck — ch<u>a</u>t　　（　　　　）

(5) b<u>ea</u>r — r<u>ea</u>listic　　（　　　　）

2 ＿＿＿＿ から最も適切な語を選び、（　　）に書き入れなさい。

(1) I have (　　　　) shoulders and want to get a massage.

(2) The students are (　　　　) to wear uniforms.

(3) Don't (　　　　) me while I am working.

(4) We enjoyed a variety of (　　　　) food.

(5) They are considering the (　　　　) of a new system.

stiff	disturb	introduction	Taiwanese	required

3 日本語に合うように、（　　）内に適切な語を入れなさい。

(1) 彼はテレビを見ながら眠ってしまった。

Watching TV, he (　　　　) (　　　　).

(2) その市の住民は計画に強く反対している。

The residents of the city are strongly (　　　　) (　　　　) the plan.

(3) もうすぐ夏休みだ。

Our summer vacation is just (　　　　) the (　　　　).

(4) 私は足りない分の知識を補わなくてはならない。

I have to (　　　　) (　　　　) for the lack of knowledge.

(5) 要するに、私は行きたくない。

(　　　　) a (　　　　), I don't want to go.

4 次の英文を読み、設問に答えなさい。

Ken: I'm ①(   ) that system because I often fall asleep in afternoon classes. According to a book I read before, we tend to feel sleepy about eight hours after waking up. Therefore, the book recommends that we should take a nap before feeling sleepy. ②Hearing about the Taiwanese custom, I'm convinced that students should take a nap after lunch. If this system were introduced, ③I wouldn't become sleepy (   ) (   ) and could focus more on afternoon classes.

Aya: Well, ④[what / I / saying / you / understand / are], Ken. But I don't think we need an afternoon nap in our school. This is because I'd prefer spending the nap time on something else. ⑤In particular, since we're graduating soon, I'd like to chat with my friends. Personally, spending time with friends is more important than sleeping.

(1) 空所①に入る最も適切な語を選び、記号で答えなさい。

    ア. against   イ. disagree   ウ. agree   エ. for   (   )

(2) 下線部②を日本語に訳しなさい。

_____

(3) 下線部③が「私はもう眠くならないだろう」という意味になるように、空所に当てはまる2語の英語を書きなさい。

_____   _____

(4) 下線部④が「あなたの言っていることはわかります」という意味になるように、[ ]内の語を並べかえなさい。

_____

(5) 下線部⑤を日本語に訳しなさい。

_____

(6) 本文の内容に合うように、次の質問に英語で答えなさい。

According to the book Ken read, when should we take a nap?

_____

5 次の英文を読み、設問に答えなさい。

Haruki: In my opinion, ① setting a nap time at school is (   ) (   )
(   ). It would be helpful to make up for my lack of sleep and
improve my concentration. University entrance exams are just around
the corner. ② Although I study a lot, I often feel it doesn't bear fruit.
That makes me feel more pressure, and I end up ③(stay) up late. As
a result, I feel sleepy the following day and can't concentrate well. It's a
vicious circle. I think a nap would make the situation better.

Mai: I understand the benefit of taking a nap after lunch. ④However, to
be honest, I don't want to take a nap, laying my head on the desk. That
would definitely cause a stiff neck or stiff shoulders. ⑤[have / effect /
afraid / it / negative / I'm / might / a] on my health. If this system
were introduced, I'd like to sleep on a bed. But it's not realistic, right?
In a nutshell, I'm against the system.

(1) 下線部①が「学校で昼寝の時間を設けることはやってみる価値がある」
という意味になるように、空所に当てはまる3語の英語を書きなさい。

_____ _____ _____

(2) 下線部②を日本語に訳しなさい。

_____

(3) ③の単語を適切な形に直しなさい。

_____

(4) 下線部④を日本語に訳しなさい。

_____

(5) 下線部⑤が「それは私の健康に悪影響があるのではないかと心配だ。」
という意味になるように、[ ]内の語を並べかえなさい。

_____ on my health.

(6) 本文の内容に合うように、次の質問に英語で答えなさい。
Does Mai agree with having a nap time at school?

_____

UNIT 3

Dog Tax

 読解のポイント

1. 犬についてどのような苦情が寄せられますか。
2. ドイツやオランダの犬税とはどのようなものですか。

Setting **Students are talking about introducing a dog tax in their city.**

Aki: Dogs are one of the most popular pets in Japan. ① They are clever and loyal to their owners. ② They can make their owners and some passersby happy. ③ On the other hand, it is true that many complaints are made about dogs. ④ For example, dogs bark loudly and might bite someone, which can make the neighbors scared. ⑤ Also, when irresponsible owners walk their dogs, they often leave the dogs' waste on the sidewalk. ⑥ What is worse, there are even owners who don't take care of their dogs or who abandon them for selfish reasons. ⑦ Thus, some measures need to be taken to promote owners' responsibility.

⑧ In fact, some cities in Germany and the Netherlands have a dog tax. The owners must pay around 100 euros for a dog per year, depending on where they live. If the owners have a second dog, they must pay more than 100 euros for that dog. ⑨ With this taxation, people are cautious about having a dog, which can make owners more responsible.

単語・語句の研究

☐ tax [tæks]	图 税
☐ loyal [lɔ́iəl]	厖 忠実な、忠誠な
☐ passersby [pæ̀sərzbái] < passerby [pæ̀sərbái]	图 通りがかりの人、通行人 参考 pass by（通り過ぎる）、-er（〜する人）
☐ complaint (s) [kəmpléint(s)]	图 苦情、クレーム
☐ loudly [láudli]	圓 大声で、騒々しく
☐ neighbor (s) [néibər(z)]	图 隣人、近所の人

☐ irresponsible [irispánsəbl]	形無責任な 参考 ir-（否定を表す接頭辞）、 responsible（責任がある）	
☐ sidewalk [sáidwɔ̀ːk]	名歩道	
☐ what is worse	その上もっと悪いことには 例 The movie is three hours long, and what is worse, it is boring.（その映画は3時間もあり、さらに悪いことに、退屈である）	
☐ **abandon** [əbǽndən]	動〜を捨てる、見捨てる	
☐ **measure (s)** [méʒər(z)]	名手段、方法	
☐ **responsibility** [rispànsəbíləti]	名責任	
☐ Netherlands [néðərləndz]	名オランダ（（ヨーロッパ北西部の国））	
☐ euro (s) [júərə(z)]	名ユーロ（（EUの共通通貨））	
☐ taxation [tækséiʃn]	名課税	
☐ **cautious** [kɔ́ːʃəs]	形用心深い、慎重な	

解説

① **They are clever and loyal to their owners.**
- They と their は前文のDogsをさす。
- clever は「利口な、賢い」、owner は「飼い主」の意味。

② **They can make their owners and some passersby happy.**
- make A B で「AをBにする」の意味。

③ **On the other hand, it is true that many complaints are made about dogs.**
- on the other hand は「他方では、これに反して」の意味。
- it is 〜 that ... は「…ということは〜だ」の意味。that節内は受け身の文になっている。make a complaint は「苦情を訴える」の意味。

④ **For example, dogs bark loudly and might bite someone, which can make the neighbors scared.**
- bark は「ほえる」、bite は「〜をかむ」、scared は「こわがった、びっくりした」の意味。

● 〈make + O + C〉は「OをC（の状態）にする」の意味。

✐確認　（　　　）内に適切な語を入れなさい。

　ア．音楽が観客をさらに興奮させた。

　　The music（　　　）the audience more（　　　）.

　イ．そのニュースは彼を怒らせた。

　　The news made（　　　）（　　　）.

⑤ **Also, when irresponsible owners walk their dogs, they often leave the dogs' waste on the sidewalk.**

● walk は「〜を散歩させる」、waste は「フン、排泄物」の意味。

⑥ **What is worse, there are even owners who don't take care of their dogs or who abandon them for selfish reasons.**

● 2つの who はどちらも関係代名詞で、who don't take care of their dogs と who abandon them for selfish reasons が先行詞 owners を後ろから修飾している。

● take care of 〜は「〜の世話をする」、selfish は「自分勝手な、わがままな」の意味。

● them は their dogs をさす。

⑦ **Thus, some measures need to be taken to promote owners' responsibility.**

● take a measure は「手段を取る、処置を講じる」の意味。ここでは need to 〜「〜する必要がある」を使った受け身の文になっている。

● to promote 〜は不定詞の副詞的用法で、「〜するために」と目的を表している。

● promote は「〜を促進する、増進する」の意味。

⑧ **In fact, some cities in Germany and the Netherlands have a dog tax.**

● some cities in Germany and the Netherlands がこの文の主語。

● tax は「税、税金」の意味。

⑨ **With this taxation, people are cautious about having a dog, which can make owners more responsible.**

● with は「〜があるので」の意味。

● which は関係代名詞（非制限用法）で、「そしてそのことは〜」と With this taxation 〜 having a dog について説明している。

読解のポイント

1. 地方自治体の首長たちは、なぜ犬税の導入を考えているのですか。
2. Bobは犬税をどのようなことに使うことができると言っていますか。

① In Japan, there used to be a dog tax in some cities until 1982. ② Today, the number of complaints about dogs is increasing. ③ So some mayors are thinking about adopting the tax to respond to such complaints.

What are your thoughts about a dog tax? ④ Should such a tax be imposed in our city?

Bob: ⑤ I think a dog tax is necessary. ⑥ With the money collected from it, the local government can take direct measures against complaints. ⑦ For example, regarding loud barking, the government can provide owners with education programs on how to discipline their dogs. ⑧ As for discarded waste, the government can place bags and trash cans on streets. ⑨ In addition, the tax can be used for protecting dogs' rights. For instance, the government can build a facility to take care of abandoned dogs. ⑩ It can help the dogs be adopted by new owners. ⑪ When dogs are abused, actions to rescue them can also be taken smoothly.

単語・語句の研究

☐ **mayor (s)** [méiər(z)]	名 市長、町長、村長	
☐ **impose (d)** [impóuz(d)]	動 （税など）を課す	
☐ **regarding** [rigá:rdiŋ]	前 ～について、～に関して	
☐ **provide ~ with ...**	～に…を提供する　例 A company provided the victims with free bread.（ある企業が被災者に無料でパンを提供した）	
☐ **discipline** [dísəplən]	動 ～をしつける	
☐ **instance** [ínstəns]	名 例	
☐ **abuse (d)** [əbjú:z(d)]	動 ～を虐待する	
☐ **rescue** [réskju:]	動 ～を救う、救助する	
☐ **smoothly** [smú:ðli]	副 円滑に、スムーズに	

解説

① **In Japan, there used to be a dog tax in some cities until 1982.**
- used to ～は「以前は～であった［していた］」の意味。ここでは there is ～「～がある」と組み合わされているので、there used to be ～は「以前は～があった」の意味。

② **Today, the number of complaints about dogs is increasing.**
- today は「今日、現在」の意味。
- the number of complaints about dogs がこの文の主語。

③ **So some mayors are thinking about adopting the tax to respond to such complaints.**
- to respond ～は不定詞の副詞的用法で、「～するために」と目的を表している。

④ **Should such a tax be imposed in our city?**
- 〈should be ＋過去分詞〉は「～されるべき」の意味。ここでは疑問文になっている。

⑤ **I think a dog tax is necessary.**
- Bob が自分の意見を述べている文。Bob は犬税の導入に賛成している。

⑥ **With the money collected from it, the local government can take direct measures against complaints.**
- with は「～があれば」、local government は「地方自治体」の意味。
- collected は過去分詞で、collected from it が the money を後ろから修飾している。

⑦ **For example, regarding loud barking, the government can provide owners with education programs on how to discipline their dogs.**
- on は「～について」、how to ～は「～の仕方、～する方法」の意味。

⑧ **As for discarded waste, the government can place bags and trash cans on streets.**

- as for 〜は「〜については、〜に関しては」、discardedは「捨てられた」、placeは「〜を置く、設置する」、trash canは「ごみ箱」の意味。

⑨ **In addition, the tax can be used for protecting dogs' rights.**

- 〈can be + 過去分詞〉は、直訳では「〜されることができる」だが、ここでは「〜することができる」と訳すほうが自然。
- 確認 （　　）内に適切な語を入れなさい。
  - ア．その鳥は沖縄で見ることができる。
    The birds (　　) (　　) seen in Okinawa.
  - イ．日本では、卵は生で食べることができる。
    Eggs can (　　) (　　) raw in Japan.
- rightは「権利」の意味。

⑩ **It can help the dogs be adopted by new owners.**

- 〈help + O + 原形不定詞〉は「Oが〜するのを助ける」の意味。ここでは原形不定詞の部分に受け身の形〈be + 過去分詞〉が入っているので、「Oが〜されるのを助ける」の意味。
- 確認 （　　）内に適切な語を入れなさい。
  - ア．ビタミンDはカルシウムが吸収されるのを助ける。
    Vitamin D (　　) calcium (　　) absorbed.
  - イ．SNSでは、ハッシュタグを使うと投稿が見つけられやすくなる。
    On social media, hashtags help posts (　　) (　　).
- adoptは「（動物など）を引き取る」の意味。

⑪ **When dogs are abused, actions to rescue them can also be taken smoothly.**

- when節は受け身の文。
- actions to rescue themが主節の主語。themはdogsをさす。
- take actionは「措置をとる」の意味。ここでは助動詞canを使った受け身の文になっている。

読解のポイント

1. Chikaは、飼い主に犬税を課すとどのようなことが起こるかもしれないと言っていますか。
2. Daisukeはテレビのニュースで何を見ましたか。

Chika: ① I don't think we need a dog tax. ② First, it's too difficult for the local government to collect the tax accurately. ③ To avoid the tax, some owners may abandon their dogs or may not register them with the city. ④ This is one of the reasons why some cities in Japan did away with a dog tax. ⑤ Furthermore, black markets may become popular, where dogs are sold and bought illegally. ⑥ Those unregistered dogs can't get proper immunizations, which creates an unhealthy environment for them. Also, what if dog owners can't afford the tax? ⑦ They might lose their jobs, or the amount of tax imposed might increase dramatically in the future. ⑧ If that happened to dog owners, they could not afford their dogs. Again, such owners would abandon their dogs.

Daisuke: ⑨ I think imposing a tax on owners is necessary. ⑩ The tax prevents them from owning too many dogs. ⑪ The other day, the TV news reported on a person who kept over 100 dogs. ⑫ The living environment of the dogs was terrible. ⑬ The neighbors said on TV that they were annoyed with the smell and noise. ⑭ If there had been a dog tax, the person might have hesitated to own so many dogs. ⑮ In general, when owners have a limited number of dogs, they can take better care of them. ⑯ As a result, the dogs' quality of life will be improved.

🅐🅑🅒 単語・語句の研究

☐ do away with 〜	〜を廃止する **例** Should our school do away with uniforms? （私たちの学校は制服を廃止すべきだろうか）
☐ black market	闇取引
☐ illegally [ilíːɡəli]	**副** 違法に **参考** il-（否定を表す接頭辞）、legally（合法的に）

☐ unregistered [ʌnrédʒistərd]	形 正式に登録されていない
	参考 un-（否定を表す接頭辞）、registered（登録済みの）
☐ immunization(s) [ìmjuːnəzéiʃn(z)]	名 予防注射
☐ **unhealthy** [ʌnhélθi]	形 健康によくない、不健康な
	参考 un-（否定を表す接頭辞）、healthy（健康的な）
☐ **annoyed** [ənɔ́id]	形 いらいらして、困って
☐ **general** [dʒénrəl]	名 一般、全般
☐ in general	一般に、たいてい
	例 In general, cats live longer than dogs.（一般に、猫は犬よりも長生きだ）

解説

① I don't think we need a dog tax.

- Chikaが自分の意見を述べている文。Chikaは犬税の導入に反対している。
- don't think (that) ～は「～ではないと思う」の意味。ここではthinkのあとに接続詞のthatが省略されている。

② First, it's too difficult for the local government to collect the tax accurately.

- it is ～ for ... to —は「…が［にとって］—するのは～だ」の意味。
- accuratelyは「正確に」の意味。

③ To avoid the tax, some owners may abandon their dogs or may not register them with the city.

- To avoid ～は不定詞の副詞的用法で、「～するために」と目的を表している。
- register ～ with ... は「～を…に登録する」の意味。
- themはtheir dogsをさす。

④ This is one of the reasons why some cities in Japan did away with a dog tax.

- whyは関係副詞で、〈reason why + S + V〉は「SがVする理由」の意味。ここではS = some cities in Japanになっている。

⑤ **Furthermore, black markets may become popular, where dogs are sold and bought illegally.**

- where は関係副詞（非制限用法）で、「そしてそこで～」と black markets について説明している。
- ✍️**確認**（　　）内に適切な語を入れなさい。
  - ア．私はチェンマイを訪れたが、そこでは毎年2月に花祭りが行われる。
    I visited Chiang Mai, (　　　) the flower festival takes place every February.
  - イ．彼らは新宿行きの電車に乗り、そこで地下鉄に乗り換えた。
    They took the train bound for Shinjuku, (　　　) (　　　) changed to the subway.

⑥ **Those unregistered dogs can't get proper immunizations, which creates an unhealthy environment for them.**

- proper は「適切な」の意味。
- which は関係代名詞（非制限用法）で、「そしてそのことは～」と Those unregistered dogs ～ immunizations について説明している。
- them は Those unregistered dogs をさす。

⑦ **They might lose their jobs, or the amount of tax imposed might increase dramatically in the future.**

- They と their は犬の飼い主たちをさす。
- the amount of tax imposed が後半の文の主語。imposed は過去分詞で、the amount of tax を後ろから修飾している。
- amount は「額、総額」、dramatically は「劇的に」の意味。

⑧ **If that happened to dog owners, they could not afford their dogs.**

- 仮定法過去の文。〈If＋S＋動詞の過去形 ～, S'＋could＋動詞の原形 …〉で「もしSが～なら、S'は…できるだろう」の意味。
- afford は「～を持つ［飼う］余裕がある」の意味。

⑨ **I think imposing a tax on owners is necessary.**

- Daisuke が自分の意見を述べている文。Daisuke は犬税の導入に賛成している。
- think のあとに接続詞の that が省略されている。imposing a tax on owners が that 節内の主語。

⑩ **The tax prevents them from owning too many dogs.**
- prevent ~ from ... は「~が…するのを妨げる」の意味。
- own は「~を所有する」の意味で、ここでは動名詞になっている。

⑪ **The other day, the TV news reported on a person who kept over 100 dogs.**
- the other day は「先日、最近」、report は「報道する」、on は「~について」の意味。
- who は関係代名詞で、who kept over 100 dogs が先行詞 a person を後ろから修飾している。

⑫ **The living environment of the dogs was terrible.**
- living environment は「生活環境」、terrible は「ひどい」の意味。

⑬ **The neighbors said on TV that they were annoyed with the smell and noise.**
- that は接続詞。said that ~は「~と言った」の意味。
- smell は「におい」、noise は「騒音」の意味。

⑭ **If there had been a dog tax, the person might have hesitated to own so many dogs.**
- 仮定法過去完了の文。〈If + S + had + 過去分詞 ~, S' + might have + 過去分詞 ...〉で「もし S が~していたら、S'は…したかもしれない」の意味。
- 確認 （　）内に適切な語を入れなさい。
  - ア．いつもの時間に家を出ていたら、私は遅刻したかもしれない。
    If I (　　) left home at the usual time, I might (　　) been late.
  - イ．数学がもっと得意だったら、彼はその試験に合格したかもしれない。
    If he had (　　) better at math, he might have (　　) the exam.

⑮ **In general, when owners have a limited number of dogs, they can take better care of them.**
- limited は「限られた」の意味。
- they は owners、them は dogs をさす。

⑯ **As a result, the dogs' quality of life will be improved.**
- as a result は「その結果（として）」、quality of life は「生活の質」の意味。

読解のポイント

教科書 p.111 *l*.5〜p.111 *l*.15

1. Eriが犬税は不公平だと言っている理由は何ですか。
2. Akiはどのような考えが気に入りましたか。

Eri: ① I see your point, but I want to emphasize that the tax is unfair. ② Dog owners may wonder why taxation applies only to dogs, not to all kinds of pets. ③ I believe that paying only a consumption tax is fair. ④ All pet owners pay a consumption tax when they buy a pet itself, pet food, and pet insurance, to name a few. That's enough. ⑤ A dog tax isn't necessary.

Aki: Well, thanks for thinking critically about a dog tax. ⑥ Your discussion gave me a lot of new perspectives. ⑦ In particular, I like the idea of improving the dogs' quality of life. I'd like to hear more opinions. So let's continue our discussion.

ABC 単語・語句の研究

☐ **insurance** [inʃúərəns]	名 保険
☐ to name a few	いくつか例を挙げれば 例 Various spices are used in Indian food, such as cumin, coriander, and turmeric, to name a few. （インド料理ではさまざまなスパイスが使われるが、いくつか例を挙げれば、クミン、コリアンダー、ターメリックがある）
☐ critically [krítikli]	副 批評的に 参考 critical（批評の）

解説

① **I see your point, but I want to emphasize that the tax is unfair.**
- thatは接続詞で、emphasize that 〜は「〜ということを強調する」の意味。
- unfairは「不公平な」の意味。

② **Dog owners may wonder why taxation applies only to dogs, not to all kinds of pets.**
- wonder why 〜は「なぜ〜なのだろうかと思う」の意味。
- 確認 （　）内に適切な語を入れなさい。
  - ア．なぜ彼女は悲しんでいるのだろう。
    I wonder (　　　) (　　　) is sad.
  - イ．私たちは、なぜバスが遅れているのだろうかと思った。
    We wondered (　　　) the bus (　　　) late.
- apply to 〜は「〜に適用される」の意味。

③ **I believe that paying only a consumption tax is fair.**
- thatは接続詞。paying only a consumption taxがthat節内の主語。
- consumption taxは「消費税」、fairは「公平な、適正な」の意味。

④ **All pet owners pay a consumption tax when they buy a pet itself, pet food, and pet insurance, to name a few.**
- theyはAll pet ownersをさす。
- a pet itselfは「ペットそのもの」、pet foodは「ペットフード」の意味。
- to name a fewはふつう文末に置く。

⑤ **A dog tax isn't necessary.**
- Eriが自分の意見を述べている文。Eriは犬税の導入に反対している。

⑥ **Your discussion gave me a lot of new perspectives.**
- discussionは「議論」、perspectiveは「観点、考え方」の意味。

⑦ **In particular, I like the idea of improving the dogs' quality of life.**
- in particularは「特に」の意味。
- idea of 〜は「〜という考え」の意味。

UNIT 3

確認問題

1 下線部の発音が同じものには○、違うものには×を（　　）に書き入れなさい。

(1) sid<u>e</u>walk — c<u>au</u>tious　　　（　　　）

(2) N<u>e</u>therlands — unh<u>ea</u>lthy　　　（　　　）

(3) imp<u>o</u>se — c<u>o</u>mfortably　　　（　　　）

(4) ab<u>a</u>ndon — p<u>a</u>sserby　　　（　　　）

(5) sm<u>oo</u>thly — imm<u>u</u>nization　　　（　　　）

2 ◻ から最も適切な語を選び、（　　）に書き入れなさい。

(1) My mother has been working for a (　　　) company for 20 years.

(2) Who is (　　　) of your city?

(3) They are always very (　　　) to their boss.

(4) I think he should take the (　　　) of the project.

(5) The drowning child was (　　　) safely.

| mayor | responsibility | rescued | insurance | loyal |

3 日本語に合うように、（　　）内に適切な語を入れなさい。

(1) ドッグトレーナーは根気強くその犬をしつけた。

The dog trainer patiently (　　　) the dog.

(2) 私が帰宅したとき、祖母は近所の人たちと話していた。

When I came home, my grandmother was talking with our (　　　).

(3) 私は彼にとてもいらいらした。

I was very (　　　) with him.

(4) 彼らは重税で苦しんだ。

They suffered from heavy (　　　).

(5) 私たちは飛行機の騒音について苦情を言った。

We made a (　　　) about the noise of planes.

4 日本語に合うように、（　　）内に適切な語を入れなさい。

(1) 彼らは私たちに食べ物を提供してくれた。

They (　　　　) us (　　　　) some food.

(2) その病気は自覚症状がなく、さらに悪いことに、進行が早い。

The disease has no obvious symptoms, and (　　　　) is (　　　　), it progresses quickly.

(3) 一般に、イギリス人は動物好きだと言われている。

(　　　) (　　　), it is said that British people are animal lovers.

(4) アメリカは1865年に奴隷制を廃止した。

The U.S. (　　　　) (　　　　) with slavery in 1865.

(5) レオナルド・ダ・ヴィンチは名画を残した。いくつか例を挙げれば、「モナ・リザ」、「最後の晩餐」、「ウィトルウィウス的人体図」だ。

Leonardo da Vinci left behind his masterpieces. "Mona Lisa", "The Last Supper", "The Vitruvian Man", (　　　) (　　　) a few.

5 次の英語を日本語に訳しなさい。

(1) I wonder why she doesn't reply to my email.

_____

(2) If he had been taller, he might have been a model.

_____

(3) I drove a car in Korea, where cars drive on the right side of the road.

_____

6 日本語に合うように、［　　］内の語句を並べかえなさい。

(1) エマからの手紙は私を幸せにした。

The letter [made / from / happy / me / Emma].

The letter _____.

(2) 街ではクリスマスソングが聞こえる。

[heard / Christmas songs / be / in / can] the city.

_____ the city.

(3) ビタミンCは鉄分が吸収されるのを助ける。

[iron / absorbed / helps / Vitamin C / be].

_____.

7 次の英文を読み、設問に答えなさい。

Aki: Dogs are one of the most popular pets in Japan. They are clever and loyal to their owners. They can make their owners and some passersby happy. ①( ) ( ) ( ) ( ), it is true that many complaints are made about dogs. For example, dogs bark loudly and might bite someone, which can make the neighbors scared. Also, when irresponsible owners walk their dogs, they often leave the dogs' waste on the sidewalk. ②( ) ( ) ( ), there are even owners who don't take care of their dogs or who abandon them for selfish reasons. Thus, some measures need to be ③(take) to promote owners' responsibility.

In fact, some cities in Germany and the Netherlands have a dog tax. The owners must pay around 100 euros for a dog per year, depending on where they live. If the owners have a second dog, they must pay more than 100 euros for that dog. ④With this taxation, people are cautious about having a dog, which can make owners more responsible.

(1) 空所①に入る最も適切な語句を選び、記号で答えなさい。

　　　ア．As soon as possible　　イ．For the first time

　　　ウ．Once upon a time　　　エ．On the other hand　　　（　　　）

(2) 空所②に入る最も適切な語句を選び、記号で答えなさい。

　　　ア．What is worse　　　　イ．At that time

　　　ウ．In my opinion　　　　エ．In recent years　　　（　　　）

(3) ③の単語を適切な形に直しなさい。

　　　_____

(4) 下線部④を日本語に訳しなさい。

　　　_____

(5) 本文の内容に合うように、次の質問に英語で答えなさい。

　　　How much must the owners pay for a second dog in some cities in Germany and the Netherlands?

　　　_____

8 次の英文を読み、設問に答えなさい。

Chika: I don't think we need a dog tax. First, it's too difficult for the local government to collect the tax accurately. To avoid the tax, some owners may abandon their dogs or may not register them with the city. ①This is one of the [some / Japan / reasons / away / why / cities / did / in] with a dog tax. ②Furthermore, black markets may become popular, where dogs are sold and bought illegally. Those unregistered dogs can't get proper immunizations, which creates an unhealthy environment for them. Also, what if dog owners can't afford the tax? They might lose their jobs, or the amount of tax imposed might increase dramatically in the future. If that happened to dog owners, they could not afford their dogs. Again, such owners would abandon their dogs.

Daisuke: I think imposing a tax on owners is necessary. The tax prevents them ③( ) owning too many dogs. The other day, the TV news reported on a person who kept over 100 dogs. The living environment of the dogs was terrible. The neighbors said on TV that they were annoyed with the smell and noise. ④If there had been a dog tax, the person might have hesitated to own so many dogs. In general, when owners have a limited number of dogs, they can take better care of them. As a result, the dogs' quality of life will be improved.

(1) 下線部①が「これは、日本のいくつかの市が犬税を廃止した理由の1つである。」という意味になるように、[ ]内の語を並べかえなさい。

This is one of the ＿＿＿＿＿＿＿＿＿＿＿＿＿＿＿＿＿＿ with a dog tax.

(2) 下線部②を日本語に訳しなさい。

＿＿＿＿＿＿＿＿＿＿＿＿＿＿＿＿＿＿＿＿＿＿＿＿＿＿＿＿＿

(3) 空所③に入る最も適切な語を選び、記号で答えなさい。

ア. for　　イ. at　　ウ. from　　エ. in　　　　　　　（　　）

(4) 下線部④を日本語に訳しなさい。

＿＿＿＿＿＿＿＿＿＿＿＿＿＿＿＿＿＿＿＿＿＿＿＿＿＿＿＿＿

(5) 本文の内容に合うように、次の質問に英語で答えなさい。

Who agrees with imposing a dog tax?

＿＿＿＿＿＿＿＿＿＿＿＿＿＿＿＿＿＿＿＿＿＿＿＿＿＿＿＿＿

Space Development

 読解のポイント

1. 人工衛星はどのような目的で使用されますか。
2. 2020年にどのようなことがありましたか。

Setting **Facts about space development are reported in a scientific magazine.**

① Space development refers to all the activities carried out by humans in space. ② It includes launching satellites and rockets, constructing a space station, and exploring planets and their moons. ③ Every year, hundreds of satellites are sent into space. ④ These satellites are utilized for various purposes, such as observing weather and improving telecommunication on the earth. ⑤ The International Space Station, which was built in 2011, orbits about 400 km above the earth now. ⑥ A variety of experiments are conducted by the staff staying on the station. ⑦ Furthermore, humans are exploring planets far away from the earth. ⑧ For example, in 2020, the Japanese space probe Hayabusa2 successfully brought back rock samples from the asteroid Ryugu after its six-year trip.

A B C 単語・語句の研究

☐ **satellite (s)** [sǽtəlàit(s)]	图 人工衛星
☐ **construct (ing)** [kənstrʌ́kt(iŋ)]	動 ～を建設する
☐ hundreds of ～	何百もの～ 例 Hundreds of birds fly to this lake every year. (毎年、何百羽もの鳥がこの湖に飛んでくる)
☐ **utilize (d)** [júːtəlàiz(d)]	動 ～を利用する
☐ telecommunication [tèləkəmjuːnəkéiʃən]	图 遠距離通信
☐ **staff** [stǽf]	图 スタッフ、職員
☐ probe [próub]	图 探測機
☐ asteroid [ǽstərɔ̀id]	图 小惑星

解説

① **Space development refers to all the activities carried out by humans in space.**

- space development は「宇宙開発」、refer to ～は「～に言及する、～を示す」の意味。
- carry out は「～を行う」の意味。ここでは過去分詞になっていて、all the activities を carried out by humans in space が後ろから修飾している。

《確認》 （　　）内に適切な語を入れなさい。

ア．博物館では、この県で発見された化石を見ることができる。
You can see fossils (　　　　) in this prefecture at the museum.

イ．今年出版された本の中で何がおすすめですか。
What would you recommend among the books (　　　) this year?

② **It includes launching satellites and rockets, constructing a space station, and exploring planets and their moons.**

- It は①の Space development をさす。
- include は「～を含む」、launch は「(ロケットなど)を打ち上げる」、space station は「宇宙ステーション」、explore は「～を探査する」、planet は「惑星」、moon は「衛星((惑星の周囲を回る天体))」の意味。
- 宇宙開発に含まれるものとして、launching satellites and rockets と constructing a space station と exploring planets and their moons の 3 つが挙げられている。

③ **Every year, hundreds of satellites are sent into space.**

- 受け身の文。sent は send「～を発射する」の過去分詞。

④ **These satellites are utilized for various purposes, such as observing weather and improving telecommunication on the earth.**

- 受け身の文。
- observe は「～を観測する」の意味。
- observing weather と improving telecommunication on the earth が、various purposes「さまざまな目的」の例として挙げられている。

⑤ **The International Space Station, which was built in 2011, orbits about 400 km above the earth now.**
- The International Space Station は「国際宇宙ステーション (ISS)」、orbit は「(人工衛星などが) 軌道を描いて回る」、about 400 km above the earth は「地球の上空約400キロメートル」の意味。
- which は関係代名詞 (非制限用法) で、which was built in 2011 が The International Space Station について説明している。
- **確認** (　) 内に適切な語を入れなさい。
  - ア. 彼らはゴールデンレトリーバーを飼っており、それは2020年生まれだ。
    They have a golden retriever, (　) was (　) in 2020.
  - イ. 首里城は火災で一部が焼失したが、現在は修復中である。
    Shuri Castle, (　) (　) partially damaged by fire, is now being restored.

⑥ **A variety of experiments are conducted by the staff staying on the station.**
- 受け身の文。
- experiment は「実験」の意味。
- staying は現在分詞で、staying on the station が the staff を後ろから修飾している。
- the station は⑤の The International Space Station のこと。

⑦ **Furthermore, humans are exploring planets far away from the earth.**
- 現在進行形の文。
- planets far away from the earth は「地球から遠く離れた惑星」の意味。

⑧ **For example, in 2020, the Japanese space probe Hayabusa2 successfully brought back rock samples from the asteroid Ryugu after its six-year trip.**
- the Japanese space probe Hayabusa2「日本の宇宙探査機『はやぶさ2』」がこの文の主語。
- successfully は「成功のうちに、うまく」、bring back ～は「～を持って帰る」、rock samples は「石のサンプル」、the asteroid Ryugu は「小惑星『リュウグウ』」の意味。
- its は Hayabusa2 をさす。

読解のポイント

1. 2019年から2021年に打ち上げられたロケットのほとんどは、どの国々のものですか。
2. 継続的にロケットを打ち上げているのはどのような国々ですか。

UNIT 3

① Since there is great potential in space, some countries are eager to explore this new frontier. ② In particular, the US, China, and Russia are competing with one another. ③ As shown in the graph, most of the rockets were launched by these three countries between 2019 and 2021. India, the EU, and Japan also launched rockets constantly. ④ The total number of rockets launched in the world is growing year by year, which demonstrates that many countries have a strong interest in space development. This trend will continue in the future.

⑤ Although there are benefits of promoting space development, it can also cause some problems. Space development is a controversial issue in modern society.

ABC 単語・語句の研究

☐ be eager to 〜	〜することを熱望している 例 The students are eager to study abroad. （その生徒たちは留学することを熱望している）
☐ **frontier** [frʌntíər]	名 未開拓の分野
☐ **graph** [grǽf]	名 グラフ
☐ **constantly** [kánstəntli]	副 絶えず、常に 参考 constant（不断の）
☐ year by year	年ごとに、年々 例 The number of traffic accidents is decreasing year by year. （交通事故の数は年々減少している）
☐ **controversial** [kàntrəvə́:rʃl]	形 議論の的になる、論争の余地がある 参考 controversy（論争）

解説

① **Since there is great potential in space, some countries are eager to explore this new frontier.**
- since は「～だから、～なので」の意味。

② **In particular, the US, China, and Russia are competing with one another.**
- in particular は「特に」、compete with ～は「～と競う」の意味。

③ **As shown in the graph, most of the rockets were launched by these three countries between 2019 and 2021.**
- 過去の受け身の文。
- as shown in ～は「～に示されるように」の意味。
- these three countries は②の the US, China, and Russia をさす。

④ **The total number of rockets launched in the world is growing year by year, which demonstrates that many countries have a strong interest in space development.**
- The total number of rockets launched in the world がこの文の主語。launched は過去分詞で、launched in the world が rockets を後ろから修飾している。
- which は関係代名詞（非制限用法）で、「そしてそのことは～」と The total number ～ year by year について説明している。
- that は接続詞で、demonstrate that ～は「～ということをはっきりと示す」の意味。
- have an interest in ～は「～に関心を持つ」の意味。

⑤ **Although there are benefits of promoting space development, it can also cause some problems.**
- although は「～だけれども」、benefit は「利益、恩恵」、promote は「～を進展させる」、cause は「～を引き起こす」の意味。

教科書 p.118

 読解のポイント

1. 宇宙開発の３つの利点とは何ですか。
2. 隕石にはどのような物質が含まれていることがありますか。

Setting **Advantages of space development are explained in a blog.**

Space development should be pushed forward for our future. ① There are at least three advantages that should be noted.

② First, humans can obtain mineral resources and new substances in space. ③ It has been found that meteorites coming from space sometimes contain minerals such as iron, nickel, and platinum. ④ This fact shows the possibility that humans can find these mineral resources on other planets. ⑤ In addition, a new substance which does not exist on the earth may be discovered. ⑥ With such a new substance, it might be possible to develop new materials and medicines.

Next, space development can lead to the advancement of technology. ⑦ For example, to improve satellites, rockets, and the space station, new technologies have been created. ⑧ These technologies have contributed to making better solar panels, water purifiers, and calculators. ⑨ Advanced technologies for space development are also useful for peoples' everyday lives.

Finally, humans can understand the earth more deeply. ⑩ It is said that water and organic substances, which are essential for life, were brought to the earth by meteorites from space. However, the truth is still unknown. ⑪ The exploration of space may help solve the mystery of how life began on the earth.

⑫ Because of these advantages, human beings should prioritize space development over all other things.

Ⓐ Ⓑ Ⓒ 単語・語句の研究

☐ push forward

〜を推し進める
例 Redevelopment is being pushed forward in the city.
（その都市では再開発が推し進められている）

☐ **meteorite (s)** [míːtiəràit(s)]　　图 隕石

☐ **nickel** [níkl]　　图 ニッケル

☐ **platinum** [plǽtənəm]　　图 プラチナ、白金

☐ **possibility** [pàsəbíləti]　　图 可能性
　　　参考 possible（可能性のある）

☐ **advancement** [ədvǽnsmənt]　　图 進歩、向上
　　　参考 advance（〜を進歩させる）

☐ **purifier (s)** [pjúərifàiər(z)]　　图 浄化装置
　　　参考 purify（〜を浄化する）

☐ **calculator (s)** [kǽlkjəlèitər(z)]　　图 計算機
　　　参考 calculate（〜を計算する）

☐ **exploration** [èkspləréiʃn]　　图 調査、探査

☐ **prioritize** [praiɔ́ːritàiz]　　動 〜を優先させる

 解説

① **There are at least three advantages that should be noted.**
- at least は「少なくとも」、advantage は「利点、メリット」の意味。
- that は関係代名詞で、that should be noted が先行詞 three advantages を後ろから修飾している。
- note は「〜を特筆する、言及する」の意味で、ここでは過去分詞になっている。〈should be ＋過去分詞〉は「〜されるべき」の意味だが、ここでは「〜すべき」と訳したほうが自然。

② **First, humans can obtain mineral resources and new substances in space.**
- obtain は「〜を得る、手に入れる」、mineral resources は「鉱物資源」の意味。

③ **It has been found that meteorites coming from space sometimes contain minerals such as iron, nickel, and platinum.**
- It は形式主語で、that 以下が真主語。
- 〈has been ＋過去分詞〉は現在完了の受け身で、「〜された」の意味。

✍確認 （　　）内に適切な語を入れなさい。

ア．その映像はフェイクだと証明された。

The video (　　　) (　　　) proven to be a fake.

イ．私のケーキは弟に食べられてしまった。

My cake has (　　　) (　　　) by my brother.

● meteorites coming from space が that 節内の主語。coming は現在分詞で、coming from space が meteorites を後ろから修飾している。

● contain は「～を含む」の意味。

④ **This fact shows the possibility that humans can find these mineral resources on other planets.**

● This fact は③全体の内容をさす。

● that は接続詞で、the possibility that ～は「～という可能性」の意味。

● these mineral resources は③の iron, nickel, and platinum をさす。

⑤ **In addition, a new substance which does not exist on the earth may be discovered.**

● which は関係代名詞で、which does not exist on the earth が先行詞 a new substance を後ろから修飾している。

● 〈may be + 過去分詞〉は「～されるかもしれない」の意味。

⑥ **With such a new substance, it might be possible to develop new materials and medicines.**

● with は「～があれば」の意味。

● such a new substance は⑤の a new substance ～ on the earth をさす。

● it は形式主語で、to develop 以下が真の主語。

● material は「原料、素材」、medicine は「薬」の意味。

⑦ **For example, to improve satellites, rockets, and the space station, new technologies have been created.**

● to improve は不定詞の副詞的用法で、to improve ～ the space station は「～するために」と目的を表している。

● 〈have been + 過去分詞〉は現在完了の受け身の文で、「～された［されてきた］」の意味。

⑧ **These technologies have contributed to making better solar panels, water purifiers, and calculators.**
- 〈have + 過去分詞〉は現在完了で、「〜した［してきた］」の意味。
- contribute to 〜は「〜に貢献する」、solar panelは「ソーラーパネル、太陽電池板」、water purifierは「浄水器」の意味。

⑨ **Advanced technologies for space development are also useful for peoples' everyday lives.**
- Advanced technologies for space developmentがこの文の主語。
- everyday life は「日常生活」の意味。

⑩ **It is said that water and organic substances, which are essential for life, were brought to the earth by meteorites from space.**
- it is said that 〜は「〜と言われている」、organic substanceは「有機物」の意味。
- whichは関係代名詞（非制限用法）で、which are essential for lifeがwater and organic substancesについて説明している。

⑪ **The exploration of space may help solve the mystery of how life began on the earth.**
- 〈help + 原形不定詞〉は「〜するのに役立つ」の意味。
- ✐確認 （　　）内に適切な語を入れなさい。
  ア. 発音の仕方を学ぶことは、リスニング能力を高めるのに役立つだろう。
  Learning how to pronounce will (　　　　) (　　　　) your listening skills.
  イ. アップサイクルはごみを減らすのに役立つ。
  Upcycling (　　　) (　　　) waste.
- how life began on the earthは間接疑問。〈how + S + V〉は「Sがどのように V するか」の意味。

⑫ **Because of these advantages, human beings should prioritize space development over all other things.**
- prioritize 〜 over ...は「...より〜を優先する」の意味。

読解のポイント

1. 宇宙開発のデメリットがいくつ書かれていますか。
2. 日本では毎年いくら宇宙開発に使われていますか。

UNIT 3

Setting **Disadvantages of space development are described in another blog.**

① Space development should not be promoted. ② The following problems need to be addressed.

First, space development requires a huge amount of money. ③ Recently, in Japan, more than 300 billion yen has been spent on space development each year. ④ Yet, space development does not necessarily achieve the desired results. ⑤ Some people argue that their governments should spend money for solving immediate problems rather than investing in faraway space.

⑥ Second, space development can damage the environment in outer space. ⑦ Broken satellites and parts of rockets, which are called space debris, remain floating around the earth. ⑧ The amount of space debris has been increasing, and scientists estimate that nearly 20,000 pieces of debris are there. ⑨ If one of these pieces hits an active satellite or the space station, it can cause a serious accident.

⑩ Third, the present situation of space development is not fair for developing countries. ⑪ Now, only rich countries compete to exploit space and to gain benefits. ⑫ Space does not belong to any country; no single country should try to dominate it.

⑬ Thus, space development brings nothing but disadvantages for humans. ⑭ It must be stopped immediately.

🅐🅑🅒 単語・語句の研究

☐ a huge amount of 〜	膨大な量の〜 例 We need to store a huge amount of data securely.（私たちは膨大な量のデータを安全に保管する必要がある）
☐ necessarily [nèsəsérəli]	副 必ず

☐ **achieve** [ətʃíːv] 　　　 　動 ～を達成する

☐ **desire (d)** [dizáiə*r*(d)] 　動 ～を強く望む

☐ **argue** [áː*r*gjuː] 　　　 　動 ～を主張する

☐ **immediate** [imíːdiət] 　　 形 目前の、当面の

☐ **invest (ing)** [invést(iŋ)] 　動 投資する

☐ **faraway** [fáːrəwèi] 　　　 形 遠くの

☐ **outer** [áutə*r*] 　　　　 　形 外の

☐ **debris** [dəbríː] 　　　　　 名 デブリ、破片、残骸

☐ **estimate** [éstəmèit] 　　　 動 ～と推定する、見積もる

☐ **exploit** [iksplɔ́it] 　　　　 動 ～を開発する

☐ **dominate** [dámənèit] 　　 動 ～を支配する

☐ **disadvantage (s)** 　　　 名 不利益、損失、デメリット
　 [dìsədvǽntidʒ(iz)]

☐ **immediately** [imíːdiətli] 　副 直ちに、すぐに

解説

① Space development should not be promoted.
- 〈should not be ＋過去分詞〉は「～されるべきではない」の意味。
- promoteは「～を促進する、奨励する」の意味で、ここでは過去分詞になっている。

② The following problems need to be addressed.
- followingは「次に述べる、以下の」の意味。
- 〈need to be ＋過去分詞〉は「～される必要がある」の意味。
- addressは「～に取り組む、対処する」の意味で、ここでは過去分詞になっている。

③ Recently, in Japan, more than 300 billion yen has been spent on space development each year.
- 300 billion yenは「3,000億円」の意味。
- 〈has been ＋過去分詞〉は現在完了の受け身の文で、「～された［されている］」の意味。

④ **Yet, space development does not necessarily achieve the desired results.**
- yetは「しかし、それにもかかわらず」、not necessarilyは「必ずしも〜でない」、desiredは「望ましい」の意味。

⑤ **Some people argue that their governments should spend money for solving immediate problems rather than investing in faraway space.**
- thatは接続詞で、argue that 〜は「〜ということを主張する」の意味。
- ... rather than 〜は「〜よりもむしろ…」の意味だが、ここではinvesting in faraway spaceよりむしろsolving immediate problemsにお金を使うべきだと述べられている。

⑥ **Second, space development can damage the environment in outer space.**
- outer spaceは「宇宙空間」の意味。

⑦ **Broken satellites and parts of rockets, which are called space debris, remain floating around the earth.**
- whichは関係代名詞（非制限用法）で、which are called space debrisがBroken satellites and parts of rocketsについて説明している。
- space debrisは「スペースデブリ、宇宙ごみ」、remainは「〜の（状態の）ままである」、floatは「漂う、浮かぶ」の意味。

⑧ **The amount of space debris has been increasing, and scientists estimate that nearly 20,000 pieces of debris are there.**
- has been 〜ingは現在完了進行形で、「（ずっと）〜し続けている」の意味。
- 確認 （　）内に適切な語を入れなさい。
  ア．彼は3時間働き続けている。
    He (　　) been (　　) for three hours.
  イ．その子猫は、母猫を探して鳴き続けている。
    The kitten (　　) (　　) meowing, looking for its mother.
- thereは⑦のaround the earthをさす。

UNIT 3

⑨ **If one of these pieces hits an active satellite or the space station, it can cause a serious accident.**
- activeは「作動中の」、causeは「〜を引き起こす」、accidentは「事故」の意味。

⑩ **Third, the present situation of space development is not fair for developing countries.**
- the present situation of space developmentがこの文の主語。
- present situationは「現状」、developing countryは「発展途上国」の意味。

⑪ **Now, only rich countries compete to exploit space and to gain benefits.**
- competeは「競う」、gainは「〜を得る」の意味。
- to exploitとto gainは不定詞の副詞的用法で、「〜するために、〜しようと」の意味。

⑫ **Space does not belong to any country; no single country should try to dominate it.**
- belong to 〜は「〜のものである」の意味。
- ;（セミコロン）は接続詞のように2つの文をつなぐ働きがあり、ここではtherefore（したがって）と同じような意味で使われている。

⑬ **Thus, space development brings nothing but disadvantages for humans.**
- nothing but 〜は「〜だけ、ただ〜のみ」の意味。

⑭ **It must be stopped immediately.**
- 〈must be＋過去分詞〉は「〜されなければならない」の意味。
- **確認** （　）内に適切な語を入れなさい。
- ア．この鏡は柔らかい布で掃除しなければならない。
    This mirror (　　) (　　) cleaned with a soft cloth.
- イ．これらのドーナツは本日中に食べなければならない。
    These donuts (　　) be (　　) today.

確認問題

1 下線部の発音が同じものには○、違うものには×を（　）に書き入れなさい。

(1) gra**ph** — sta**ff**　　　（　　　）

(2) pri**o**ritize — pr**o**be　　　（　　　）

(3) m**e**teorite — imm**e**diate　　　（　　　）

(4) **a**rgue — **ou**ter　　　（　　　）

(5) calculat**o**r — platin**u**m　　　（　　　）

2 ‾‾‾ から最も適切な語を選び、（　）に書き入れなさい。

(1) There is a (　　　) of snow today.

(2) We should (　　　) more money in real estates.

(3) They (　　　) water power to produce electricity.

(4) Azuchi Castle was (　　　) on flat land.

(5) He called the police (　　　).

| constructed | possibility | immediately | utilize | invest |

3 日本語に合うように、（　）内に適切な語を入れなさい。

(1) 電気自動車のデメリットの１つは、充電するのに時間がかかることだ。

One of the (　　　) of electric vehicles is that they take time to be recharged.

(2) 彼女は英語のテストで目標を達成するために努力した。

She tried hard to (　　　) her goal on the English test.

(3) これは宇宙から来た謎の生物の物語だ。

This is a story of a mysterious creature from (　　　) space.

(4) 長い間、死刑制度は議論を呼ぶ問題である。

The death penalty has been a (　　　) issue for a long time.

(5) だいちは地球を観測するために2006年に打ち上げられた人工衛星だ。

Daichi is a (　　　) launched in 2006 to observe the earth.

4 日本語に合うように、(　　)内に適切な語を入れなさい。

(1) プレミアリーグの選手たちには膨大な額の金が支払われる。

A (　　　) (　　　) of money is paid to the Premier League players.

(2) 20世紀後半に、経済のグローバル化が推し進められた。

In the late 20th century, economic globalization was (　　　) (　　　).

(3) その都市では、観光客の数が年々増加している。

In the city, the number of tourists has been increasing (　　　) (　　　) year.

(4) 何百人もの生徒が校庭に集まった。

(　　　) (　　　) students gathered in the schoolyard.

(5) モリス夫妻は息子に会うことを熱望している。

Mr. and Mrs. Morris are (　　　) (　　　) see their son.

5 次の英語を日本語に訳しなさい。

(1) We have been watching the game from the beginning.

_____

(2) Taking a bath helps improve the quality of your sleep.

_____

(3) Jupiter, which has 95 moons, is the largest planet in the solar system.

_____

6 日本語に合うように、[　　]内の語を並べかえなさい。

(1) その歌手の新曲が今日発売された。

The singer's [been / new / released / song / has] today.

The singer's _____ today.

(2) この知識は全員に共有されなければならない。

This [with / must / shared / knowledge / be] everyone.

This _____ everyone.

(3) 生徒たちによって描かれた花の絵が飾られていた。

Pictures of [the / painted / students / flowers / by] were on display.

Pictures of _____ were on display.

7 次の英文を読み、設問に答えなさい。

Space development refers to all the activities carried out by humans in space. ①It includes launching satellites and rockets, constructing a space station, and exploring planets and their moons. Every year, hundreds of satellites are ②(send) into space. These satellites are utilized for various purposes, such as observing weather and improving telecommunication on the earth. ③The International Space Station, which was built in 2011, orbits about 400 km above the earth now. A variety of experiments are conducted by the staff ④(stay) on the station. Furthermore, ⑤humans are exploring planets (   ) (   ) (   ) the earth. For example, in 2020, the Japanese space probe Hayabusa2 successfully brought back rock samples from the asteroid Ryugu after its six-year trip.

(1) 下線部①を日本語に訳しなさい。

_____

(2) ②の単語を適切な形に直しなさい。

_____

(3) 下線部③を日本語に訳しなさい。

_____

(4) ④の単語を適切な形に直しなさい。

_____

(5) 下線部⑤が「人間は地球から遠く離れた惑星を調査している」という意味になるように、空所に当てはまる3語の英語を書きなさい。

_____ _____ _____

(6) 本文の内容に合うように、次の質問に英語で答えなさい。
What did Hayabusa2 successfully bring back from Ryugu?

_____

8 次の英文を読み、設問に答えなさい。

Space development should not be promoted. The following problems need to be addressed.

First, space development requires a huge amount of money. ①Recently, in Japan, more than 300 billion yen has been spent on space development each year. Yet, space development does not necessarily achieve the desired results. Some people argue that ②their governments should spend money for [problems / than / solving / investing / rather / immediate] in faraway space.

Second, space development can damage the environment in outer space. Broken satellites and parts of rockets, which are called space debris, remain floating around the earth. The amount of space debris has been increasing, and scientists estimate that nearly 20,000 pieces of debris are there. If one of these pieces hits an active satellite or the space station, it can cause a serious accident.

Third, the present situation of space development is not fair for ③( ) ( ). Now, only rich countries compete to exploit space and to gain benefits. Space does not belong to any country; no single country should try to dominate it.

Thus, space development brings nothing but disadvantages for humans. It must be stopped immediately.

(1) 下線部①を日本語に訳しなさい。

(2) 下線部②が「政府は遠くの宇宙に投資するよりも、目前の問題を解決するためにお金を使うべきだ」という意味になるように、[ ]内の語を並べかえなさい。
their governments should spend money on ＿＿＿＿＿＿＿＿＿＿＿
＿＿＿＿＿＿＿＿＿＿＿＿＿＿＿＿ in faraway space

(3) 空所③に入る最も適切な語句を選び、記号で答えなさい。
ア．the earth　　　　　　イ．developing countries
ウ．developed countries　　エ．outer space　　　　　　（　　）

(4) 本文の内容に合うように、次の質問に英語で答えなさい。
What are broken satellites and parts of rockets in outer space called?
＿＿＿＿＿＿＿＿＿＿＿＿＿＿＿＿＿＿＿＿＿＿＿＿＿＿＿＿＿

Anne of Green Gables

 読解のポイント

1. マリラはグリーン・ゲイブルズをどうしようとしていますか。
2. アンはマリラの言葉にどのように反応していますか。

₁ One afternoon, Marilla came slowly in from the front yard where she had been talking to a caller.

₂ "What did that man want, Marilla?"

Marilla sat down by the window and looked at Anne. ₃ There were tears in her eyes and her voice broke as she said:

₄ "He heard that I was going to sell Green Gables, and he wants to buy it."

₅ "Buy it! Buy Green Gables?" ₆ Anne wondered if she had heard aright. ₇ "Oh, Marilla, you don't mean to sell Green Gables!"

"₈ Anne, I don't know what else is to be done. ₉ I've thought it all over. ₁₀ If my eyes were strong, I could stay here and make out to look after things and manage, with a good hired man. ₁₁ But as it is, I can't. I may lose my sight altogether; and anyway, I'll not be healthy to run things. ₁₂ Oh, I never thought I'd live to see the day when I'd have to sell my home. ₁₃ But things would only go worse and worse all the time. ₁₄ If it would be sold, it won't bring much. The land is small, and the buildings are old. ₁₅ But it'll be enough for me to live on, I reckon. ₁₆ I'm thankful you're provided with that scholarship, Anne. ₁₇ I'm sorry you won't have a home to come back in your vacations, that's all I'm worried about, but I suppose you'll manage somehow."

Marilla broke down and wept bitterly.

"You mustn't sell Green Gables," said Anne decisively.

₁₈ "Oh, Anne, I wish I didn't have to. But you can see for yourself. I can't stay here alone. ₁₉ I'd go crazy with trouble and loneliness. ₂₀ And my sight would go — I know it would."

🅰🅱🅲 単語・語句の研究

☐ Anne [ǽn]	图 アン《人名》
☐ Green Gables [gríːn géiblz]	グリーン・ゲイブルズ《マリラやアンの家》
☐ Marilla [mərílə]	图 マリラ《人名》
☐ caller [kɔ́ːlər]	图 訪問者
☐ voice broke	声を詰まらせた
☐ aright [əráit]	副 正しく
☐ make out	うまくやる
☐ **hire (d)** [háiər(d)]	動 〜を雇う、雇用する
☐ **sight** [sáit]	图 視力
☐ lose one's sight	視力を失う
☐ **altogether** [ɔ̀ːltəgéðər]	副 完全に、全く
☐ run things	物事をやりくりする
☐ thankful [θǽŋkfl]	形 感謝している
☐ **scholarship** [skálərʃip]	图 奨学金
☐ **somehow** [sʌ́mhàu]	副 何とかして、どうにかして
☐ break down	取り乱す
☐ **wept** [wépt] (< **weep** [wíːp])	動 涙を流す、泣く
☐ **bitterly** [bítərli]	副 激しく
☐ decisively [disáisivli]	副 きっぱりと、断固として
☐ loneliness [lóunlinəs]	图 寂しさ、孤独

🗨 解説

① **One afternoon, Marilla came slowly in from the front yard where she had been talking to a caller.**

- Marilla「マリラ」は、主人公のAnne「アン」を孤児院から引き取って育てた女性。アンたちはカナダのプリンス・エドワード島で暮らしている。Reading ①では、『赤毛のアン』の最後の章が扱われている。
- where は関係副詞で、where she had been talking to a callerが先行詞 the front yard を後ろから修飾している。
- ⟨had been 〜ing⟩ は過去完了進行形で、「(ずっと)〜していた」の意味。

② **"What did that man want, Marilla?"**
- ● アンのセリフ。
- ● that manは①のa callerをさす。

③ **There were tears in her eyes and her voice broke as she said:**
- ● tearは「涙」、asは「〜のとき」の意味。
- ● :（コロン）は、人物のセリフを続けるときにも使われる。

④ **"He heard that I was going to sell Green Gables, and he wants to buy it."**
- ● マリラのセリフ。
- ● Heは②のthat manをさす。
- ● thatは接続詞で、heard that 〜は「〜ということを聞いた」の意味。
- ● Green Gables「グリーン・ゲイブルズ」は「緑の切妻屋根」の意味で、マリラやアンが住んでいる家のこと。

⑤ **"Buy it! Buy Green Gables?"**
- ● アンのセリフ。マリラの言ったことに驚いて、繰り返している。

⑥ **Anne wondered if she had heard aright.**
- ● wonderは「〜だろうかと思う」、ifは「〜かどうか」の意味。
- ● 〈had + 過去分詞〉は過去完了で、「〜した」の意味。

⑦ **"Oh, Marilla, you don't mean to sell Green Gables!"**
- ● アンのセリフ。
- ● mean to 〜は「〜するつもり」の意味。

⑧ **Anne, I don't know what else is to be done.**
- ● ⑧〜⑰はマリラのセリフ。
- ● what else is to be doneのwhatは疑問詞と考えられる。elseは「ほかに」、be to 〜は「〜すべき」の意味。be to 〜はここではis to 〜になっており、be doneという受け身〈be + 過去分詞〉が続いている。したがって、what else is to be doneは「ほかに何をすべきか」の意味。

⑨ **I've thought it all over.**
- ● 〈have + 過去分詞〉は現在完了で、「〜した」の意味。

⑩ **If my eyes were strong, I could stay here and make out to look after things and manage, with a good hired man.**
- If my eyes were strong「私の目が健康なら」とあるが、マリラはこのままでは失明する可能性があるので目に負担のかかることは控えるように医師から言われている。
- 仮定法過去の文。〈If S + 動詞の過去形 〜, S' + could + 動詞の原形 ...〉で「もしSが〜なら、S'は…できるだろう」の意味。
- look after 〜は「〜の世話をする」、manage は「暮らしていく」の意味。
- マリラの兄のマシューが主に農場の仕事をしていたが、マシューは突然亡くなってしまったため、マリラは with a good hired man「よい人を雇って」と言っている。

⑪ **But as it is, I can't.**
- as it is は「実際のところは」の意味。

⑫ **Oh, I never thought I'd live to see the day when I'd have to sell my home.**
- I never thought I'd live to see the day when 〜は「私は〜する日が来るとは思ってもみなかった」の意味。
- when は関係副詞で、when I'd have to sell my home が先行詞 the day を後ろから修飾している。
- I'd はどちらも I would の短縮形。

⑬ **But things would only go worse and worse all the time.**
- 〈比較級 + and + 比較級〉は「ますます〜」の意味なので、go worse and worse は「どんどん悪化する」ということ。
- all the time は「絶えず、常に」の意味。

⑭ **If it would be sold, it won't bring much.**
- it は Green Gables をさす。
- it would be sold は受け身の文。
- much は「多額」の意味で、it won't bring much は「たいした金額にはならないだろう」ということ。

⑮ **But it'll be enough for me to live on, I reckon.**
- it は形式主語で、to live on が真主語。live on は「生き延びる」の意味。
- reckon は「思う」の意味。

⑯ **I'm thankful you're provided with that scholarship, Anne.**

- thankfulのあとに接続詞のthatが省略されている。
- provide 〜 with ... は「〜に…を提供する」の意味で、ここでは受け身になっている。
- that scholarship「あの奨学金」とは、アンがレドモンド大学へ進学するために獲得した、クイーンズ学院の奨学金のこと。

⑰ **I'm sorry you won't have a home to come back in your vacations, that's all I'm worried about, but I suppose you'll manage somehow.**

- sorryとsupposeのあとに接続詞のthatが省略されている。
- to come backは不定詞の形容詞的用法。a home to come backで「帰ってくる(ための)家」の意味。
- that's all I'm worried aboutは「それだけが心配だ」、supposeは「〜と思う、推測する」、manageは「うまくやっていく」の意味。

⑱ **Oh, Anne, I wish I didn't have to.**

- ⑱〜⑳はマリラのセリフ。
- 仮定法過去の文。〈I wish + S + 動詞の過去形 〜〉は「Sが〜ならいいのに」の意味。
- *確認* (　)内に適切な語を入れなさい。

  ア．もっとあなたと話す時間があればいいのに。

  　 I (　　) I (　　) more time to talk with you.

  イ．もっと泳ぎがうまかったらなあ。

  　 I (　　) I (　　) a better swimmer.
- have toのあとにsell Green Gablesが省略されている。

⑲ **I'd go crazy with trouble and loneliness.**

- if節はないが、If I stayed here alone「もしここに1人でいるなら」が省略された仮定法過去の文と考えると理解しやすい。
- I'dはI would の短縮形。
- go crazy with 〜は「〜でおかしくなる」、troubleは「苦労」の意味。

⑳ **And my sight would go — I know it would.**

- itはmy sightをさす。2つめのwouldのあとにもgoが省略されている。

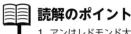 **読解のポイント**

1. アンはレドモンド大学へ行かずに何をすると言っていますか。
2. アンの計画を聞いて、マリラはどのように反応していますか。

"You won't have to stay here alone, Marilla. I'll be with you. ① I'm not going to Redmond University."

"Not going to Redmond!" ② Marilla lifted her worn face from her hands and looked at Anne. "Why, what do you mean?"

"③ Just what I say. I'm not going to take the scholarship. ④ I decided so the night after you came home from the hospital. ⑤ You surely don't think I could leave you alone in your trouble, Marilla, after all you've done for me. ⑥ I've been thinking and planning. ⑦ Let me tell you my plans. ⑧ Mr. Barry wants to rent the farm for next year. So you won't have any bother over that. And I'm going to teach. ⑨ I've applied for the Carmody School and was accepted. ⑩ But the school was a bit far from here. ⑪ Then I found out that Gilbert Blythe has kindly decided to let me teach at the Avonlea School in our neighborhood. So I can live with you. ⑫ Oh, I have it all planned out, Marilla. ⑬ And I'll read to you and keep you cheered up. ⑭ You shall not be dull or lonesome. ⑮ And we'll be real cozy and happy here together, you and I."

⑯ Marilla had listened like a woman in a dream.

"⑰ Oh, Anne, I could get on real well if you were here, I know. ⑱ But I can't let you sacrifice yourself so much for me. It would be terrible."

ᴬᴮᶜ 単語・語句の研究

☐ Redmond [rédmənd]	名 レドモンド ((架空の大学の名前))	
☐ Barry [bǽri]	名 バリー ((姓))	
☐ rent [rént]	動 ～を借りる、賃借する	
☐ **bother** [bάðər]	名 悩みの種	
☐ bother over ～	～についての悩み	
	例 I have a bother over my future course. （私には進路についての悩みがある）	

☐ apply for ~	～に申し込む 例 She applied for the job. （彼女はその仕事に応募した）
☐ Carmody [kάːrmədi]	名 カーモディ（（架空の町の名前））
☐ Gilbert Blythe [gílbərt bláið]	名 ギルバート・ブライス（（人名））
☐ **kindly** [káindli]	副 快く、好意的に
☐ Avonlea [ǽvənli]	名 アヴォンリー（（架空の村の名前））
☐ keep ~ cheered up	～を常に元気づける 例 He kept his friends cheered up. （彼は友だちを常に元気づけた）
☐ lonesome [lóunsəm]	形 寂しい、孤独な
☐ cozy [kóuzi]	形 くつろいだ、和気あいあいとした
☐ get on real well	とてもうまくやっていく
☐ **sacrifice** [sǽkrəfàis]	動 ～を犠牲にする

 解説

① I'm not going to Redmond University.

- アンのセリフ。
- 現在進行形の否定文。ここでは未来のことを表すために現在進行形が使われている。

② Marilla lifted her worn face from her hands and looked at Anne.

- lift は「（顔など）を上げる」、worn は「やつれた、疲れた」の意味。

③ Just what I say.

- ③～⑮はアンのセリフ。
- Just what I say. は「（私が）言った通りのこと」の意味。

④ I decided so the night after you came home from the hospital.

- so は「そのように」の意味。「そのように決めた」＝「レドモンド大学に行かないと決めた」ということ。
- the night after you came home from the hospital は「あなたが病院から帰ってきた夜」の意味。マリラが眼科医に診てもらった日のこと。

⑤ **You surely don't think I could leave you alone in your trouble, Marilla, after all you've done for me.**
- think のあとに接続詞の that が省略されている。
- 〈leave + O + alone〉は「O を孤独にする」の意味。
- after all you've done for me は「あなたが私のためにいろいろとしてくれたのに」の意味。

⑥ **I've been thinking and planning.**
- 〈have been ～ing〉は現在完了進行形で、「(ずっと)～している、～してきた」の意味。

⑦ **Let me tell you my plans.**
- 〈let + O + 原形不定詞〉は「O に～させる」の意味。

⑧ **Mr. Barry wants to rent the farm for next year.**
- Mr. Barry は、アンの親友ダイアナ・バリーの父のこと。
- farm は「農場」の意味。

⑨ **I've applied for the Carmody School and was accepted.**
- 〈have + 過去分詞〉は現在完了で、「～した」の意味。
- the Carmody School「カーモディの学校」は架空の小学校。
- accept は「～を受け入れる」の意味で、ここでは受け身の文なので過去分詞になっている。

⑩ **But the school was a bit far from here.**
- a bit は「少し」、far from ～ は「～から遠い」の意味。

⑪ **Then I found out that Gilbert Blythe has kindly decided to let me teach at the Avonlea School in our neighborhood.**
- find out that ～ は「～ということがわかる」の意味。
- Gilbert Blythe「ギルバート・ブライス」はアンの同級生。
- 〈let + O + 原形不定詞〉は「O に～させる」の意味。
- the Avonlea School「アヴォンリーの学校」は架空の小学校で、アンたちの母校。ギルバートはここで教師をすることになっていたが、アンに職を譲ってくれた。

⑫ **Oh, I have it all planned out, Marilla.**
- it と all は同格の関係。
- plan out は「〜を計画する」の意味。

⑬ **And I'll read to you and keep you cheered up.**
- read to 〜は「〜に(本などを)読んで聞かせる」の意味。アンは朗読が得意。

⑭ **You shall not be dull or lonesome.**
- dull は「元気のない、活力のない」の意味。

⑮ **And we'll be real cozy and happy here together, you and I.**
- この real は副詞で「本当に」の意味。

⑯ **Marilla had listened like a woman in a dream.**
- 〈had + 過去分詞〉は過去完了で、「〜した」の意味。

⑰ **Oh, Anne, I could get on real well if you were here, I know.**
- マリラのセリフ。
- 仮定法過去の文。〈If + S + 動詞の過去形 〜, S' + could + 動詞の原形 ...〉で「もし S が〜なら、S'は…できるだろう」の意味。ここでは if 節が後半に来ている。

  📝**確認**　(　　)内に適切な語を入れなさい。
  ア．自転車を持っていれば、簡単に図書館に行けるのに。
  　　If I (　　　) a bike, I (　　　) go to the library easily.
  イ．もしこのコンピュータがもっと安ければ買えるのに。
  　　If this computer (　　　) cheaper, I could (　　　) it.

⑱ **But I can't let you sacrifice yourself so much for me.**
- マリラのセリフ。
- 〈let + O + 原形不定詞〉は「O に〜させる」の意味。

読解のポイント

1. アンは勉強を続けるのをあきらめましたか。
2. アンは自分の将来についてどのような比喩で表現していますか。

"Nonsense!" Anne laughed merrily. "There is no sacrifice. ① <u>Nothing could be worse than giving up Green Gables — nothing could hurt me more.</u> ② <u>We must keep the dear old place.</u> ③ <u>My mind is quite made up, Marilla.</u> ④ <u>I'm *not* going to Redmond; and I *am* going to stay here and teach.</u> Don't worry about me a bit."

"But your ambitions and ...."

"I'm just as ambitious as ever. ⑤ <u>Only, I've changed the object of my ambitions.</u> I'm going to be a good teacher, and I'm going to save your eyesight. ⑥ <u>Besides, I mean to study at home here and take a little college course all by myself.</u> Oh, I've dozens of plans, Marilla. I've been thinking them out for a week. ⑦ <u>I shall give life here my best, and I believe it will give its best to me in return.</u> ⑧ <u>When I left Queen's Academy, my future seemed to stretch out before me like a straight road.</u> I thought I could see many milestones along it. Now there is a bend in it. ⑨ <u>I don't know what lies around the bend, but I'm going to believe that the best does.</u> ⑩ <u>It has a fascination of its own, that bend, Marilla.</u> ⑪ <u>I wonder how the road beyond it goes."</u>

A B C 単語・語句の研究

☐ **nonsense** [nánsens]	圏 ばかな、くだらない	
☐ **ambition (s)** [æmbíʃn(z)]	图 念願、大望	
☐ **as ～ as ever**	いつものように～だ 例 Our teacher is as busy as ever. （私たちの先生はいつものように忙しい）	
☐ **ambitious** [æmbíʃəs]	形 大望のある、野心のある	
☐ **dozen (s)** [dʌ́zn(z)]	图 ダース、12個	
☐ dozens of ～	たくさんの～ 例 I have dozens of stuffed animals. （私はたくさんのぬいぐるみを持っている）	

☐ think ~ out	～をよく考える 例 You need to think things out. （あなたは物事をよく考える必要がある）
☐ in return	お返しに 例 I gave her a present in return for her help. （助けてくれたお返しに、私は彼女にプレゼントを贈った）
☐ Queen's Academy	クイーン学院（（アンが卒業した学校））
☐ **stretch** [strétʃ]	動（道などが）広がる、延びている
☐ stretch out	広がる 例 The sea stretched out before us. （私たちの前には海が広がっていた）
☐ milestone (s) [máilstòun(z)]	名（道しるべを示す）マイル標石
☐ **bend** [bénd]	名 曲がり角、カーブ
☐ fascination [fæsənéiʃn]	名 魅力 参考 fascinate（～を魅了する）

UNIT 3

 解説

① **Nothing could be worse than giving up Green Gables — nothing could hurt me more.**
- ①～⑪はアンのセリフ。
- Nothing could be worse than ～は「～より悪いことはない」、nothing could hurt ～ moreは「～をより傷つけることはない」の意味。アンにとって、グリーン・ゲイブルズを手放すことは何よりもいやだということ。
- give upは「～を引き渡す、譲る」の意味。

② **We must keep the dear old place.**
- dearは「大事な」の意味。the dear old placeはGreen Gablesをさす。

③ **My mind is quite made up, Marilla.**
- make up one's mindは「決心する」の意味。ここではmy mindが主語の受け身の文になっている。

④ I'm *not* going to Redmond; and I *am* going to stay here and teach.
- I'm *not* going to Redmondは現在進行形の文だが、未来のことを表している。

⑤ Only, I've changed the object of my ambitions.
- onlyは「ただ〜だけ」、objectは「対象、目標」の意味。
- 〈have + 過去分詞〉は現在完了で、「〜した」の意味。

⑥ Besides, I mean to study at home here and take a little college course all by myself.
- mean to 〜は「〜するつもりである」、college courseは「大学の課程」、all by oneselfは「独力で、ひとりで」の意味。

⑦ I shall give life here my best, and I believe it will give its best to me in return.
- give life here my bestは「ここでの生活に全力を尽くす」の意味。
- believeのあとに接続詞のthatが省略されている。itやitsはlife here「ここでの生活」をさす。

⑧ When I left Queen's Academy, my future seemed to stretch out before me like a straight road.
- seem to 〜は「〜するように思われる」の意味。

⑨ I don't know what lies around the bend, but I'm going to believe that the best does.
- whatは疑問詞と解釈できる。what lies around the bendは「その曲がり角を曲がったところに何があるか」の意味。
- thatは接続詞で、believe that 〜は「〜ということを信じる」の意味。

⑩ It has a fascination of its own, that bend, Marilla.
- Itはthat bendをさす。

⑪ I wonder how the road beyond it goes.
- 〈wonder + how + S + V〉は「どのようにSはVするだろうか」の意味。ここではS = the road beyond it「その先の道」、V = goesである。itは⑩のthat bendをさす。つまり、how the road beyond it goesは「その（曲がり角の）先の道はどのようになっているか」の意味。

読解のポイント

教科書 p.128 *l*.1〜p.128 *l*.18

1. ダイアナはどのような合図をアンに送りましたか。
2. アンは「お化けの森」で何とつぶやきましたか。

① "I don't want to let you give it up," said Marilla, referring to the scholarship.

"But you can't prevent me. ② I'm sixteen and a half, 'obstinate as a mule,' as Mrs. Lynde once told me," laughed Anne.

"③ Oh, Marilla, don't you go pitying me. ④ I don't like to be pitied, and there is no need for it. ⑤ I'm glad over the very thought of staying at dear Green Gables. ⑥ Nobody could love it as you and I do, so we must keep it."

⑦ "You blessed girl!" said Marilla, yielding. ⑧ "I feel as if you'd given me new life. ⑨ I guess I ought to stick out and make you go to college — but I know I can't, so I'm not going to try. I'll make it up to you though, Anne."

⑩ A light flashed in the window at Orchard Slope, Diana's house near Green Gables.

⑪ "Diana is signaling for me to come over," laughed Anne. ⑫ "You know we keep up the old custom since we were young. ⑬ Excuse me while I run over and see what she wants."

⑭ Anne ran down the hill like a deer and disappeared in the firry shadows of the Haunted Wood.

⑮ "Dear old world," she murmured, "you are very lovely, and I am glad to be alive in you."

単語・語句の研究

☐ obstinate [ábstənət]	形 頑固な、強情な
☐ mule [mjúːl]	名 ラバ ((オスのロバとメスの馬との子))
☐ obstinate as a mule	ラバみたいに頑固
☐ Lynde [líind]	名 リンド ((姓))
☐ **pity (ing)** [píti(iŋ)]	動 〜をかわいそうに思う、哀れむ
☐ You blessed girl!	なんとありがたい子なんだろう！

☐ stick out	最後まで続ける 例 He stuck out to pass the exam. （彼は試験に合格するために最後までがんばった）
☐ I'll make it up to you though, Anne.	この埋め合わせはするからね、アン。
☐ Orchard Slope [ɔ́ːrtʃərd slóup]	オーチャード・スロープ（（ダイアナの家））
☐ Diana [daiǽnə]	名 ダイアナ（（人名））
☐ **signal (ing)** [sígnəl(in)]	動 合図する
☐ firry [fə́ːri]	形 モミの
☐ the firry shadows of the Haunted Wood	「お化けの森」にあるモミの木陰
☐ haunt (ed) [hɔ́ːnt(id)]	動 （幽霊などが）〜に出没する
☐ **murmur (ed)** [mə́ːrmər(d)]	動 ささやく、つぶやく

 解説

① **"I don't want to let you give it up," said Marilla, referring to the scholarship.**
- ●〈let ＋ O ＋原形不定詞〉は「Oに〜させる」の意味。
- ● it は the scholarship をさす。
- ● referring to 〜は分詞構文で、ここでは「〜しながら」の意味。
- ● refer to 〜は「〜に言及する」の意味。

② **I'm sixteen and a half, 'obstinate as a mule,' as Mrs. Lynde once told me," laughed Anne.**
- ●後の as は「〜（する）通りに」の意味。
- ● Mrs. Lynde「リンド夫人」はアンたちの近所に住む女性。

③ **Oh, Marilla, don't you go pitying me.**
- ● don't you go 〜ing は「〜（するような真似は）しないで」の意味。

④ **I don't like to be pitied, and there is no need for it.**
- ● be pitied は受け身の形。to be pitied は「かわいそうだと思われること」の意味。

- there is no need for ～は「～の必要はない」の意味。
- it は pitying me をさす。

⑤ **I'm glad over the very thought of staying at dear Green Gables.**

- over は「～について」、very は「ただ～だけで」の意味。

⑥ **Nobody could love it as you and I do, so we must keep it.**

- it はどちらも Green Gables をさす。
- as は「(…が)～するように」の意味。
- do は代動詞で、love の代わりに使われている。

⑦ **"You blessed girl!" said Marilla, yielding.**

- blessed は「ありがたい、喜ばしい」の意味。
- yield は「屈する、負ける」の意味。ここでは分詞構文で、「～して、そして」の意味。マリラはアンの考えに従うことにしたということ。

⑧ **I feel as if you'd given me new life.**

- as if ～は「あたかも(～する)かのように」の意味。主節 (I feel) より前の事柄について述べているので、as if 節 (as if you'd given me new life) は仮定法過去完了の文になっている。you'd は you had の短縮形。
- 確認 ( ) 内に適切な語を入れなさい。
   ア．彼女はその事件について、まるで昨日起こったかのように話した。
  She talked about the incident (　　　) (　　　) it had happened yesterday.
  イ．彼の顔はまるでハチに刺されたかのように腫れていた。
  His face was swollen as (　　　) he (　　　) been stung by a bee.

⑨ **I guess I ought to stick out and make you go to college — but I know I can't, so I'm not going to try.**

- I guess と I know のあとに接続詞の that が省略されている。
- ought to ～は「～すべきである」、〈make + O + 原形不定詞〉は「O に～させる」の意味。

⑩ **A light flashed in the window at Orchard Slope, Diana's house near Green Gables.**

- flashは「ぴかっと光る」の意味。アンとダイアナは、夜は窓辺でろうそくをちらちらと光らせてコミュニケーションを取っている。
- Orchard SlopeとDiana's house near Green Gablesは同格の関係。

⑪ **"Diana is signaling for me to come over," laughed Anne.**

- signal to 〜は「〜するように合図する」、come overは「やって来る」の意味。

⑫ **You know we keep up the old custom since we were young.**

- You knowのあとに接続詞のthatが省略されている。
- keep upは「(慣習など)を維持する、続ける」の意味。

⑬ **Excuse me while I run over and see what she wants.**

- run overは「急いで行く」の意味。
- whatは疑問詞で、what she wantsは「彼女が何を欲しているか＝彼女の用は何か」の意味。sheはDianaをさす。

⑭ **Anne ran down the hill like a deer and disappeared in the firry shadows of the Haunted Wood.**

- hillは「丘」、deerは「鹿」の意味。
- the Haunted Wood「お化けの森」は、グリーン・ゲイブルズとオーチャード・スロープの間にある森のこと。アンは想像力豊かな少女で、湖や森などに独特の名前をつけている。

⑮ **"Dear old world," she murmured, "you are very lovely, and I am glad to be alive in you."**

- aliveは「生きている」の意味。

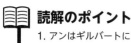 読解のポイント

1. アンはギルバートにどのようなことを伝えましたか。
2. ギルバートは勉強を続けるつもりですか。

① The following day, on her way back from Matthew's grave, Anne came across a tall lad whistling. ② It was Gilbert, and the whistle died on his lips as he recognized Anne. ③ He lifted his cap courteously, but he would have passed on in silence, if Anne had not stopped and held out her hand.

④ "Gilbert," she said, with scarlet cheeks, "I want to thank you for giving up the school for me. ⑤ It was very kind of you, and I want you to know that I appreciate it."

Gilbert took the offered hand eagerly.

"It wasn't particularly kind of me at all, Anne. ⑥ I was pleased to be able to do you some small service. ⑦ Are we going to be friends after this? ⑧ Have you really forgiven me my old fault?"

⑨ Anne laughed and tried unsuccessfully to withdraw her hand.

"⑩ I forgave you that day by the pond landing, although I didn't know it. ⑪ What a stubborn little goose I was. I may as well make a complete confession. ⑫ I've been sorry ever since."

"We are going to be the best of friends," said Gilbert, joyfully. "We were born to be good friends, Anne. I know we can help each other in many ways. You are going to keep up your studies, aren't you? ⑬ So am I. Come, I'm going to walk home with you."

ABC 単語・語句の研究

☐ Matthew [mǽθjuː]	名	マシュー ((人名))
☐ grave [gréiv]	名	墓
☐ lad [lǽd]	名	青年
☐ whistling [hwíslɪŋ] (< whistle)	動	口笛を吹く
☐ courteously [kə́ːrtiəsli]	副	礼儀正しく、丁寧に
☐ pass on		通り過ぎる

☐ in silence	黙って
☐ **silence** [sáiləns]	图 沈黙、無言
☐ hold out ~	～を差し出す
	例 He held out his cup for more tea. (彼は紅茶のお代わりを求めてカップを差し出した)
☐ scarlet [skάːrlət]	形 緋色 ((明るい赤色)) の
☐ eagerly [íːgərli]	副 熱心に
☐ **particularly** [pərtíkjələrli]	副 特に、とりわけ
☐ **forgive (n)** [fərgív(n)]	動 ～を許す
☐ **fault** [fɔ́ːlt]	图 誤り、過失
☐ old fault	昔の過ち ((ギルバートがアンの赤毛をからかったこと))
☐ unsuccessfully [ʌnsəksésfəli]	副 失敗して
☐ **withdraw** [wiðdrɔ́ː]	動 (手など)を引っ込める
☐ the pond landing	池の船着き場
☐ **stubborn** [stʌ́bərn]	形 頑固な、強情な
☐ goose	(やや古)あほう、ばか
☐ may as well ~	～したほうがよい
	例 We may as well go out in the morning. (私たちは午前中に出かけたほうがよい)
☐ **confession** [kənféʃn]	图 白状、告白
☐ joyfully [dʒɔ́ifəli]	副 うれしそうに、喜んで
☐ be born to be ~	生まれながら～である
	例 She was born to be a poet. (彼女は生まれながらの詩人だ)

 解説

① **The following day, on her way back from Matthew's grave, Anne came across a tall lad whistling.**

- the following day は「翌日」、on one's way back from ~ は「～からの帰り道で」、come across ~ は「～に出くわす、偶然会う」の意味。
- Matthew「マシュー」はマリラの兄。アンはマシューとマリラといっしょに暮らしていた。

- whistle はここでは現在分詞になっており、a tall lad を後ろから修飾している。

② **It was Gilbert, and the whistle died on his lips as he recognized Anne.**
- It は①の a tall lad whistling をさす。
- whistle は「口笛」、die は「次第に消える」、as は「〜するとき」、recognize は「〜がだれであるかわかる」の意味。

③ **He lifted his cap courteously, but he would have passed on in silence, if Anne had not stopped and held out her hand.**
- but のあとは仮定法過去完了の文。〈If + S + had + 過去分詞 〜, S' + would have + 過去分詞 ...〉で「もし S が〜したら、S' は…しただろう」の意味。ここでは if 節が否定文で、後半に来ている。
- 確認 （　）内に適切な語を入れなさい。
  ア．あなたが誘ってくれなかったら、私は他の部に入っていただろう。
    If you (　　) not asked me to join you, I (　　) have joined another club.
  イ．ギルバートがアンをニンジンと呼んでいなかったら、2人は親友になっていただろう。
    If Gilbert had not called Anne carrots, they (　　) (　　) become fast friends.

④ **"Gilbert," she said, with scarlet cheeks, "I want to thank you for giving up the school for me.**
- cheek は「頬」の意味。
- the school は the Avonlea School をさす。

⑤ **It was very kind of you, and I want you to know that I appreciate it.**
- アンのセリフ。
- it was very kind of you は「どうもご親切に」、appreciate は「〜を感謝する」の意味。
- 〈want + O + to + 動詞の原形〉は「O に〜してほしい」の意味。
- I appreciate it の it は④の giving up the school for me をさす。

⑥ **I was pleased to be able to do you some small service.**
- ⑥～⑧はギルバートのセリフ。
- pleasedは「うれしい」、do O a serviceは「Oの手助けをする」の意味。

⑦ **Are we going to be friends after this?**
- after thisは「今後は」の意味。

⑧ **Have you really forgiven me my old fault?**
- 現在完了〈have + 過去分詞〉の疑問文。「～しましたか」の意味。
- forgive O_1 O_2は「O_1のO_2を許す」の意味。ここではO_1 = me、O_2 = my old faultである。
- 11歳のときに、ギルバートはアンの赤毛をからかった。

⑨ **Anne laughed and tried unsuccessfully to withdraw her hand.**
- unsuccessfullyは「失敗して」の意味。ギルバートがアンの手を握ったままだったので、引っ込められなかったということ。

⑩ **I forgave you that day by the pond landing, although I didn't know it.**
- ⑩～⑫はアンのセリフ。
- that day by the pond landingは、13歳のアンが小舟に乗って遊んでいたら浸水してしまったところをギルバートが助けてくれたときのこと。
- itはI forgave youをさす。

⑪ **What a stubborn little goose I was.**
- 〈What a + 形容詞 + 名詞 + S + V〉の形の感嘆文。「Sはなんて～な…なのだろう」の意味。

⑫ **I've been sorry ever since.**
- 現在完了〈have + 過去分詞〉の文。「(ずっと)～している」の意味。
- ever since「それ以来ずっと」とは、⑩のthat dayをさす。

⑬ **So am I.**
- 〈so + V + S〉は「SもVする、Sも同じだ」の意味。ここではI am going to keep up my studies, too. と同じ意味。

読解のポイント

1. アンとギルバートが話しているのを見て、マリラはどのように反応しましたか。
2. アンはどのような気持ちで窓辺に座りましたか。

UNIT 3

Marilla looked curiously at Anne when she entered the kitchen.

① "Who was that who came up the lane with you, Anne?"

② "Gilbert Blythe," answered Anne, who found herself blushing. ③ "I met him on Barry's hill."

④ "I didn't think you and Gilbert Blythe were such good friends that you'd stand for half an hour at the gate talking to him," said Marilla with a dry smile.

"⑤ We haven't been good friends, rather we've been good enemies. ⑥ But we have decided that it will be much more sensible to be good friends in the future. Were we really there half an hour? It seemed just a few minutes. ⑦ But, you see, we have five years' lost conversations to catch up with, Marilla."

⑧ Anne sat long at her window that night companioned by a glad content. ⑨ The wind blew softly in the cherry branches, and the smell of mint came up to her. The stars twinkled over the pointed firs.

⑩ Anne's horizons had closed in since the night she had sat there after coming home from Queen's Academy; but if the path set before her feet was to be narrow, she knew that flowers of quiet happiness would bloom along it. And there was always the bend in the road!

⑪ "'God's in his heaven, all's right with the world,'" whispered Anne softly.

単語・語句の研究

☐ curiously [kjú(ə)riəsli]	副 興味ありげに **参考** curious（好奇心の強い）
☐ lane [léin]	名 小道、細道
☐ blush (ing) [bláʃ(iŋ)]	動 顔を赤らめる

☐ such ~ that ...	…であるほど～だ 例 The ramen shop is such a popular one that there is always a long line.（そのラーメン店は常に長蛇の列ができるほどの人気店だ）
☐ **sensible** [sénsəbl]	形 賢明な
☐ be sensible to ~	～するのは賢明である
☐ catch up with ~	～に追いつく 例 I'm studying hard to catch up with my classmates.（私はクラスメイトに追いつくために、一生懸命勉強している）
☐ **companion (ed)** [kəmpǽnjən(d)]	動 ～に付き添う、伴う
☐ **content** [kəntént]	名 満足、安心感
☐ **softly** [sɔ́ːftli]	副 優しく、穏やかに 参考 soft（穏やかな）
☐ **branch (es)** [brǽntʃ(iz)]	名 枝
☐ **twinkle (d)** [twíŋkl(d)]	動 （星などが）きらきら光る
☐ the pointed fir	尖ったモミ
☐ **fir (s)** [fə́ːr(z)]	名 モミ
☐ close in	狭くなる
☐ the bend in the road	道の曲がり角
☐ "God's in his heaven, all's right with the world,"	（（ロバート・ブラウニングの詩からの引用））

解説

① **"Who was that who came up the lane with you, Anne?"**
- 初めのWhoは疑問詞で、who came up ～のwhoは関係代名詞。who came up with the lane with youが先行詞thatを後ろから修飾している。

② **"Gilbert Blythe," answered Anne, who found herself blushing.**
- whoは関係代名詞（非制限用法）で、「そしてその人［彼女］は～」とAnneについて説明している。
- 確認 （　　）内に適切な語を入れなさい。
   ア．ダイアナはオーチャード・スロープに住んでおり、アンの親友だ。
   Diana, (　　) (　　) in Orchard Slope, is Anne's best friend.

イ．アンは、パフスリーブのドレスをくれたマシューに感謝した。

Anne was grateful to Matthew, (　　　) (　　　) her a puff-sleeved dress.

● 〈find + O + C〉は「OがCであるとわかる、気づく」の意味。

③ "I met him on Barry's hill."

● アンのセリフ。
● Barry's hillは「バリー家の丘」の意味。

④ "I didn't think you and Gilbert Blythe were such good friends that you'd stand for half an hour at the gate talking to him," said Marilla with a dry smile.

● thinkのあとに接続詞のthatが省略されている。
● you'dはyou wouldの短縮形。
● stand ～ingは「～しながら立つ」の意味で、ここではfor half an hour at the gateが間に挟まっている。

⑤ We haven't been good friends, rather we've been good enemies.

● ⑤～⑦はアンのセリフ。
● We haven't been good friendsは、現在完了〈have + 過去分詞〉の否定文。「（ずっと）～ではなかった」の意味。
● ratherは「それどころか」、enemyは「敵、ライバル」の意味。
● we've been good enemiesは現在完了〈have + 過去分詞〉の文。「（ずっと）～だった」の意味。

⑥ But we have decided that it will be much more sensible to be good friends in the future.

● 現在完了〈have + 過去分詞〉の文。「～した」の意味。
● thatは接続詞で、decided that ～は「～であると判断した」の意味。
● that節内のitは形式主語で、to be good friendsが真の主語。

⑦ But, you see, we have five years' lost conversations to catch up with, Marilla.

● you seeは「ほらね、あのね」という意味のつなぎ言葉。
● to catch up withは不定詞の形容詞的用法で、「～するための、～すべき」の意味。five years' lost conversations「5年間もの失われた会話」を後ろから修飾している。

⑧ **Anne sat long at her window that night companioned by a glad content.**

- sat は sit「座る」の過去形。long は「長く、長い間」の意味。

⑨ **The wind blew softly in the cherry branches, and the smell of mint came up to her.**

- blew は blow「吹く」の過去形。
- cherry は「桜」、branch は「枝」、come up to ～は「～に達する、届く」の意味。

⑩ **Anne's horizons had closed in since the night she had sat there after coming home from Queen's Academy; but if the path set before her feet was to be narrow, she knew that flowers of quiet happiness would bloom along it.**

- Anne's horizons had closed in ～は過去完了〈had + 過去分詞〉の文。「～した」の意味。
- horizon は「地平線」の意味。
- she had sat there ～ from Queen's Academy が the night を後ろから修飾している。she had sat は過去完了〈had + 過去分詞〉の文。there は at her window をさす。
- the path set before her feet が if 節の主語。set は set「～を配置する」の過去分詞で、set before her feet が the path を後ろから修飾している。
- 〈be 動詞 + to + 動詞の原形〉は「～することになっている、～する予定だ」の意味。ここでは was to be と過去形になっている。
- that は接続詞で、flowers of quiet happiness が that 節の主語。
- bloom は「咲く、開花する」の意味。
- it は the path set before her feet をさす。
- クイーンズ学院から帰ってきた日には、奨学金を獲得して大学にも進学できる状況だったが、マシューの死やマリラの目の悪化などでアンの進路は変わってしまった。しかし、アンは前向きな気持ちを持っている。

⑪ **"'God's in his heaven, all's right with the world,'" whispered Anne softly.**

- 'God's in his heaven, all's right with the world,' はロバート・ブラウニングの「朝の詩」からの引用。「神は天に在り、この世はすべてよし」の意味。

確認問題

1 下線部の発音が同じものには○、違うものには×を（　　）に書き入れなさい。

(1) w<u>ee</u>p — <u>ea</u>gerly 　　（　　　　）

(2) f<u>au</u>lt — withdr<u>aw</u> 　　（　　　　）

(3) h<u>i</u>re — p<u>i</u>ty 　　（　　　　）

(4) c<u>o</u>zy — c<u>o</u>nfession 　　（　　　　）

(5) st<u>u</u>bborn — d<u>o</u>zen 　　（　　　　）

2 ＿＿＿ から最も適切な語を選び、（　　）に書き入れなさい。

(1) She （　　　　） her favorite song.

(2) I visited my family's （　　　　） last week.

(3) A girl joyfully ran down the （　　　　）.

(4) He （　　　　） me for being late.

(5) My sister has good （　　　　） and doesn't need to wear glasses.

sight	forgave	whistled	grave	lane

3 日本語に合うように、（　　）内に適切な語を入れなさい。

(1) あなたは休憩したほうがよい。

You may （　　　　） （　　　　） have a break.

(2) 彼は黙って息子の話を聞いた。

He listened to his son （　　　　） （　　　　）.

(3) 私たちはそのツアーに申し込みたいです。

We'd like to （　　　　） （　　　　） the tour.

(4) そのフィギュアスケーターは、スタンディングオベーションを受けるほどすばらしい演技をした。

The figure skater gave （　　　　） a wonderful performance （　　　　） she received a standing ovation.

(5) 彼は立ち上がって手を差し出した。

He stood up and （　　　　） （　　　　） his hand.

4 次の英文を読み、設問に答えなさい。

"You won't have to stay here alone, Marilla. I'll be with you. I'm not going to Redmond University."

"Not going to Redmond!" Marilla lifted her worn face from her hands and looked at Anne. "Why, what do you mean?"

"Just what I say. I'm not going to take the scholarship. I decided ①so the night after you came home from the hospital. You surely don't think I could leave you alone in your trouble, Marilla, after all you've done for me. I've been thinking and planning. Let me tell you my plans. Mr. Barry wants to rent the farm for next year. So you won't have any bother over that. And I'm going to teach. I've applied for the Carmody School and was accepted. But the school was a bit far from here. Then I found out that Gilbert Blythe has kindly ②(decide) to let me teach at the Avonlea School in our neighborhood. So I can live with you. Oh, I have it all planned out, Marilla. And ③I'll read to you [up / you / and / cheered / keep]. You shall not be dull or lonesome. And we'll be real cozy and happy here together, you and I."

Marilla had listened like a woman in a dream.

"Oh, Anne, ④I could get on real well if you were here, I know. But I can't let you sacrifice yourself so much for me. It would be terrible."

(1) 下線部①がさす内容を、本文中から6語で抜き出して書きなさい。

　　_____.

(2) ②の単語を適切な形に直しなさい。

　　_____

(3) 下線部③が「私があなたに本を読んで、常に元気づけてあげる。」という意味になるように、[ ]内の語を並べかえなさい。
　　I'll read to you _____.

(4) 下線部④を日本語に訳しなさい。

　　_____

(5) 本文の内容に合うように、次の質問に英語で答えなさい。
　　Who wants to rent the farm for next year?

　　_____

5 次の英文を読み、設問に答えなさい。

The following day, on her way back from Matthew's grave, Anne came across a tall lad whistling. It was Gilbert, and the whistle died on his lips as he recognized Anne. He lifted his cap courteously, but ①he would have passed on in silence, if Anne had not stopped and held out her hand.

"Gilbert," she said, with scarlet cheeks, "I want to thank you for giving up the school for me. It was very kind of you, and ②[to / want / that / know / I / you] I appreciate it."

Gilbert took the offered hand eagerly.

"It wasn't particularly kind of me at all, Anne. I was pleased to be able to do you some small service. Are we going to be friends after this? Have you really ③(forgive) me my old fault?"

Anne laughed and tried unsuccessfully to withdraw her hand. "I forgave you that day by the pond landing, although I didn't know it. What a stubborn little goose I was. I may as well make a complete confession. I've been sorry ever since."

"We are going to be the best of friends," said Gilbert, joyfully. "④We were ( ) ( ) ( ) good friends, Anne. I know we can help each other in many ways. You are going to keep up your studies, aren't you? So am I. Come, I'm going to walk home with you."

(1) 下線部①を日本語に訳しなさい。

_____

(2) 下線部②が「私はそれを感謝しているということをあなたに知ってほしい」という意味になるように、[ ]内の語を並べかえなさい。

_____ I appreciate it

(3) ③の単語を適切な形に直しなさい。　_____

(4) 下線部④が「私たちは生まれながらの親友だ」という意味になるように、空所に当てはまる3語の英語を書きなさい。

_____ _____ _____

(5) 本文の内容に合うように、次の質問に英語で答えなさい。
Is Gilbert going to keep up his studies?

_____

Rules are Rules?

 読解のポイント

1. フラナリー氏とモアハウス氏は何をめぐって口論していますか。
2. モアハウス氏は運送費がいくらだと主張していますか。

₁ Mike Flannery, the agent of the Interurban Express Company, leaned over the counter in the company's office in Westcote and shook his fist. ₂ Mr. Morehouse, angry and red, stood on the other side of the counter, shaking with fury. ₃ The argument had been long and hot. ₄ At last Mr. Morehouse had become speechless.

₅ The cause of the trouble lay on the counter between the two men. ₆ It was a box with two guinea pigs inside.

₇ "Do as you like, then!" shouted Flannery. "₈ Pay for them and take them. Or don't pay for them and leave them here. Rules are rules, Mr. Morehouse. ₉ And Mike Flannery is not going to break them."

₁₀ "What are you talking about?" shouted Mr. Morehouse, madly shaking a thin book beneath the agent's nose. ₁₁ "Can't you read it here — in your own book of transportation rates? ₁₂ 'Pets, domestic, Franklin to Westcote, if properly boxed, twenty-five cents each.'"

単語・語句の研究

☐ Mike Flannery [máik flǽnəri]	图 マイク・フラナリー ((人名))
☐ **agent** [éidʒənt]	图 係員
☐ Interurban Express Company [intərə́:rbən-]	图 インターアーバン・エクスプレス・カンパニー ((会社名)) 参考 interurban (都市間の)、express (運送業)
☐ **counter** [káuntər]	图 カウンター、勘定台
☐ Westcote [wéstkòut]	图 ウエストコート ((駅名))
☐ **fist** [físt]	图 握りこぶし

☐ Morehouse [mɔ́:*r*hàus]	名 モアハウス((姓))	
☐ fury [fjúəri]	名 激しい怒り	
☐ speechless [spíːtʃləs]	形 口がきけない	
☐ guinea pig (s) [gíni pìg(z)]	ギニーピッグ((テンジクネズミ。日本ではモルモットと呼ばれる))	
☐ pay for ～	～の支払いをする 例 Let me pay for lunch. (昼食代は私に払わせてください)	
☐ madly [mǽdli]	副 激しく、取り乱して 参考 mad(発狂している)	
☐ beneath [biníːθ]	前 ～の下の	
☐ domestic [dəméstik]	形 人に飼育されている	
☐ Franklin [frǽŋklən]	名 フランクリン((駅名))	
☐ properly [prápə*r*li]	副 適切に 参考 proper(適切な)	

UNIT 3

解説

① **Mike Flannery, the agent of the Interurban Express Company, leaned over the counter in the company's office in Westcote and shook his fist.**

- Mike Flannery と the agent of the Interurban Express Company は同格の関係。
- lean は「寄りかかる、もたれる」の意味。
- shook は shake「振り回す」の過去形。

② **Mr. Morehouse, angry and red, stood on the other side of the counter, shaking with fury.**

- angry and red の前に非制限用法の who was を入れて、Mr. Morehouse, who was angry and red, ～「モアハウス氏は怒って赤くなっており、～」とすると理解しやすい。
- shaking with fury は分詞構文で、「～しながら」の意味。shake with fury は「怒りで震える」の意味。

🖊**確認** (　　)内に適切な語を入れなさい。

ア．彼女は音楽を聞きながら、歩いて駅に向かっていた。

She was walking to the station, (　　　) to music.

イ．トムはリサとおしゃべりしながら教室に入ってきた。

Tom came into the classroom, (　　　) with Lisa.

③ **The argument had been long and hot.**

● 過去完了〈had＋過去分詞〉の文。

🖊**確認** (　　)内に適切な語を入れなさい。

ア．これらの犬たちは捨てられていた。

These dogs had (　　　) abandoned.

イ．私たちは昨年までオーストラリアに住んでいた。

We (　　　) (　　　) in Australia until last year.

④ **At last Mr. Morehouse had become speechless.**

● 過去完了〈had＋過去分詞〉の文。

⑤ **The cause of the trouble lay on the counter between the two men.**

● lay は lie「ある」の過去形。

● the two men はフラナリー氏とモアハウス氏をさす。

⑥ **It was a box with two guinea pigs inside.**

● It は⑤の The cause of the trouble をさす。

● a box with ～ inside は「～が入っている箱」の意味。

⑦ **"Do as you like, then!" shouted Flannery.**

● as は「～する通りに」の意味なので、Do as you like は「好きにしなさい」ということ。

● shout は「叫ぶ、大声で言う」の意味。

⑧ **Pay for them and take them.**

● ⑧と⑨はフラナリー氏のセリフ。

● them はどちらも two guinea pigs をさす。

⑨ **And Mike Flannery is not going to break them.**

　● them は前文の rules をさす。

⑩ **"What are you talking about?" shouted Mr. Morehouse, madly shaking a thin book beneath the agent's nose.**

　● madly shaking a thin book ～は分詞構文で、「～しながら」の意味。

　● shake はここでは「～を振る、揺する」、thin は「薄い」の意味。

　● the agent はフラナリー氏をさす。

⑪ **Can't you read it here — in your own book of transportation rates?**

　● ⑪と⑫はモアハウス氏のセリフ。

　● Can't you ～? は「あなたは～できないのですか」の意味で、いらいらしたりあきれたりしているときに使う表現。

　● transportation rates は「運送費」の意味。

⑫ **'Pets, domestic, Franklin to Westcote, if properly boxed, twenty-five cents each.'**

　● モアハウス氏は、フランクリンから送られてきたペット用のギニーピッグを受け取ろうとしている。

　● if properly boxed は if のあとに they are が省略されている受け身の文と考えればよい。box は「～を箱に入れる、詰める」の意味。

　● cent は「セント（通貨単位）」の意味。twenty-five cents each は「１匹につき25セント」ということ。

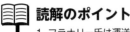 **読解のポイント**

1. フラナリー氏は運送費がいくらだと主張していますか。
2. モアハウス氏はギニーピッグを受け取りましたか。

① He threw the book on the counter. "What more do you want? ② Aren't they pets? Aren't they domestic? Aren't they properly boxed? What?"

③ He turned and walked back and forth rapidly, with a furious look on his face. "Pets," he said. "P-E-T-S! Twenty-five cents each. Two times twenty-five is fifty! Can you understand that? I offer you fifty cents."

Flannery reached for the book. ④ He ran his hand through the pages and stopped at page sixty-four.

"I won't accept fifty cents," he whispered in an unpleasant voice. "⑤ Here's the rule for it: 'When the agent is in any doubt about which of two rates should be charged on a shipment, he shall charge the larger. ⑥ The person receiving the shipment may put in a claim for the overcharge.' In this case, Mr. Morehouse, I am in doubt. ⑦ Those animals may be pets. ⑧ And they may be domestic, but I'm sure they are pigs. And the rulebook says clearly, 'Pigs, Franklin to Westcote, thirty cents each.'"

Mr. Morehouse shook his head bluntly. "Nonsense!" he shouted. "Complete nonsense, I tell you! That rule means common pigs, not guinea pigs!"

"Pigs are pigs," Flannery said firmly.

⑨ Mr. Morehouse bit his lip and then flung his arms out wildly. "Very well!" he shouted. "You shall hear of this! ⑩ Your president shall hear of this! It is an outrage! I have offered you fifty cents. You refuse it. Keep the pigs until you are ready to take the fifty cents. ⑪ But, if one hair of those pigs' heads is harmed, I will have the law on you!" ⑫ He turned and walked out, slamming the door. Flannery carefully lifted the box from the counter and put it in a corner.

Ⓐ Ⓑ Ⓒ 単語・語句の研究

☐ threw [θrúː] (< **throw**)　　　勔 ～を投げる

☐ forth [fɔ́ːrθ]　　　副 前へ

☐ rapidly [rǽpidli]	副 すばやく	
☐ **furious** [fjúəriəs]	形 猛烈に怒った	
☐ two times twenty-five	25かける2	
☐ reach for 〜	〜に手をのばす 例 He reached for the hat on the shelf.(彼は棚の上の帽子に手をのばした)	
☐ **unpleasant** [ʌnpléznt]	形 不快にさせる、いやな	
☐ rate (s) [réit(s)]	名 割合，比率	
☐ be in doubt	疑問がある	
☐ which of two rates should be charged	2つの料金のどちらが課されるべきか	
☐ **charge (d)** [tʃɑ́ːrdʒ(d)]	動 (料金などを)〜に請求する	
☐ shipment [ʃípmənt]	名 発送品	
☐ put in a claim for 〜	〜を要求する 例 The employees put in a claim for a wage increase.(従業員たちは賃上げを要求した)	
☐ overcharge [óuvərtʃɑ̀ːrdʒ]	名 不当な値段、過剰請求	
☐ rulebook [rúːlbùk]	名 規則集	
☐ bluntly [blʌ́ntli]	副 ぶっきらぼうに、無遠慮に	
☐ I tell you!	本当に！	
☐ firmly [fɚ́ːrmli]	副 断固として	
☐ flung [flʌ́ŋ] (< **fling** [flíŋ])	動 (両腕を)急に伸ばす	
☐ **wildly** [wáildli]	副 乱暴に、荒々しく	
☐ Very well!	(納得していないが)結構だ！	
☐ You shall hear of this!	君はこのままでは済まないぞ！	
☐ outrage [áutrèidʒ]	名 侮辱	
☐ **harm (ed)** [hɑ́ːrm(d)]	動 〜を傷つける	
☐ I will have the law on you!	警察を呼ぶぞ！	
☐ **slam (ming)** [slǽm(iŋ)]	動 (戸など)をばたんと閉める	

解説

① **He threw the book on the counter.**

● He はモアハウス氏をさす。

② **Aren't they pets?**
- モアハウス氏のセリフ。
- theyはギニーピッグをさす。

③ **He turned and walked back and forth rapidly, with a furious look on his face.**
- lookは「表情」の意味。

④ **He ran his hand through the pages and stopped at page sixty-four.**
- Heはフラナリー氏をさす。
- ranはrun「(指など)を走らせる」の過去形。

⑤ **Here's the rule for it: 'When the agent is in any doubt about which of two rates should be charged on a shipment, he shall charge the larger.**
- ⑤〜⑧はフラナリー氏のセリフ。

⑥ **The person receiving the shipment may put in a claim for the overcharge.**
- The person receiving the shipmentがこの文の主語。receiving the shipmentがThe personを後ろから修飾している。

⑦ **Those animals may be pets.**
- Those animalsはギニーピッグをさす。

⑧ **And they may be domestic, but I'm sure they are pigs.**
- theyはどちらもギニーピッグをさす。

⑨ **Mr. Morehouse bit his lip and then flung his arms out wildly.**
- bitはbite「〜を噛む」の過去形。

⑩ **Your president shall hear of this!**
- ⑩と⑪はモアハウス氏のセリフ。
- presidentは「社長」の意味。

⑪ **But, if one hair of those pigs' heads is harmed, I will have the law on you!**
- if節は受け身の文で、one hair of those pigs' headsが主語。

⑫ **He turned and walked out, slamming the door.**
- slamming the doorは分詞構文で、「〜して、そして」の意味。

読解のポイント

1. モアハウス氏の手紙に対して、請求係からはどのような返事が来ましたか。
2. フラナリー氏は、ギニーピッグが何匹になっているのを発見しましたか。

① Mr. Morehouse quickly wrote a letter to the president of the transportation express company. ② The president answered, informing Mr. Morehouse that all claims for overcharge should be sent to the Claims Department.

Mr. Morehouse wrote to the Claims Department. One week later he received an answer. ③ The Claims Department said it had discussed the matter with the agent at Westcote. ④ The agent said Mr. Morehouse had refused to accept the two guinea pigs shipped to him. ⑤ Therefore, the department said, Mr. Morehouse had no claim against the company and should write to its Tariff Department.

Mr. Morehouse wrote to the Tariff Department. ⑥ He stated his case clearly. ⑦ The head of the Tariff Department read Mr. Morehouse's letter. "Huh! Guinea pigs," he said. "Probably starved to death by this time." ⑧ He wrote to the agent asking why the shipment was held up. ⑨ He also wanted to know if the guinea pigs were still in good health.

⑩ Before answering, Agent Flannery wanted to make sure his report was up to date. ⑪ So he went to the back of the office and looked into the cage. Good Lord! ⑫ There were now eight of them! ⑬ All well and eating like hippopotamuses.

⑭ He went back to the office and explained to the head of the Tariff Department what the rules said about pigs. ⑮ And as for the condition of the guinea pigs, said Flannery, they were all well. ⑯ But there were eight of them now, all good eaters.

単語・語句の研究

☐ **inform (ing)** [infɔ́ːrm(iŋ)]　　動 〜に知らせる

☐ Claims Department　　　　請求係

☐ tariff [tǽrəf]	图 料金	
☐ Tariff Department	料金係	
☐ huh [hʌ́]	圃 ふん、へえ ((驚きなどを表す))	
☐ starve to death	飢え死にする 囲 Many people starved to death in the war. （その戦争では多くの人々が餓死した）	
☐ be in good health	健康である 囲 My grandmother is in good health. （私の祖母は健康です）	
☐ up to date	更新されている 囲 The software is up to date. （そのソフトウェアは最新のものだ）	
☐ look into ～	～をのぞきこむ	
☐ cage [kéidʒ]	图 かご、ケージ	
☐ lord [lɔ́ːrd]	图 神、キリスト	
☐ Good Lord!	おやまあ！	
☐ eater (s) [íːtər(z)]	图 食べる生き物	

 解説

① **Mr. Morehouse quickly wrote a letter to the president of the transportation express company.**
- transportation express company は「運送会社」の意味で、the transportation express company は「インターアーバン・エクスプレス・カンパニー」をさす。

② **The president answered, informing Mr. Morehouse that all claims for overcharge should be sent to the Claims Department.**
- informing Mr. Morehouse that ～は分詞構文で、「～して、そして」の意味。
- that は接続詞で、inform that ～は「～を告げる」の意味。that 節は all claims for overcharge が主語で、〈should be + 過去分詞〉「～されるべきだ」という受け身の文になっている。claim は「請求」の意味。

③ **The Claims Department said it had discussed the matter with the agent at Westcote.**
- said のあとに接続詞の that が省略されている。

- that節は過去完了〈had + 過去分詞〉の文で、主語のit は The Claims Department をさす。discuss は「〜について話し合う、相談する」の意味。
- the agent at Westcote はフラナリー氏をさす。

④ **The agent said Mr. Morehouse had refused to accept the two guinea pigs shipped to him.**
- The agent は③の the agent at Westcote をさす。
- said のあとに接続詞の that が省略されている。
- that節は過去完了〈had + 過去分詞〉の文。refuse to 〜は「〜することを拒む」の意味。
- ship は「〜を送る」の意味で、ここでは過去分詞になっており、shipped to him が the two guinea pigs を後ろから修飾している。him は Mr. Morehouse をさす。

⑤ **Therefore, the department said, Mr. Morehouse had no claim against the company and should write to its Tariff Department.**
- the department は③の The Claims Department をさす。
- its は the company をさす。the company とはインターアーバン・エクスプレス・カンパニーのこと。

⑥ **He stated his case clearly.**
- He は前文の Mr. Morehouse をさす。
- state は「〜をはっきり述べる」、case は「問題」の意味。

⑦ **The head of the Tariff Department read Mr. Morehouse's letter.**
- head は「(部局などの) 長、頭」の意味。

⑧ **He wrote to the agent asking why the shipment was held up.**
- write 〜ing は「〜するために手紙を書く」の意味。
- 〈why + S + V〉は「S が V する理由」の意味。ここでは why のあとが受け身の文になっている。hold up は「〜を遅らせる」の意味。

🖋確認 ( ) 内に適切な語を入れなさい。

ア. あなたは私たちが Z 世代と呼ばれている理由を知っていますか。

Do you know ( ) ( ) are called Generation Z?

UNIT 3

イ．私が遅刻した理由を説明させてください。

Let me explain (　　　) (　　　) was late.

● the agentはフラナリー氏をさす。

⑨ **He also wanted to know if the guinea pigs were still in good health.**

● ifは「～かどうか」の意味。if以下がknowの目的語になっている。

⑩ **Before answering, Agent Flannery wanted to make sure his report was up to date.**

● before ～ingは「～する前に」の意味。

● make sureのあとに接続詞のthatが省略されている。make sure that ～は「～ということを確かめる」の意味。

● hisはAgent Flanneryをさす。

⑪ **So he went to the back of the office and looked into the cage.**

● look into ～は「～の中をのぞく」の意味。

⑫ **There were now eight of them!**

● themはギニーピッグをさす。eight of themは「8匹のギニーピッグ」の意味。

⑬ **All well and eating like hippopotamuses.**

● 文頭にThey wereが省略されている。

● wellは「健康な」、hippopotamusは「カバ」の意味。

⑭ **He went back to the office and explained to the head of the Tariff Department what the rules said about pigs.**

● go back to ～は「～に戻る」の意味。

● what the rules said about pigsは間接疑問。〈what + S + V〉で「Sは何をVするか」の意味。sayは「～と書いてある」の意味。

🖋**確認**　(　　　)内に適切な語を入れなさい。

ア．あなたが昨日何を食べたか教えてください。

Please tell me (　　　) you (　　　) yesterday.

イ．私は自分が何をすべきかわかっています。

I know (　　　) (　　　) should do.

198

⑮ **And as for the condition of the guinea pigs, said Flannery, they were all well.**

 ● as for ～は「～について」、conditionは「状態」の意味。

 ● theyはthe guinea pigsをさす。

⑯ **But there were eight of them now, all good eaters.**

 ● all good eatersはand they were all good eatersと解釈できる。ギニーピッ
 グはみなエサをよく食べているということ。

読解のポイント

1. 社長はギニーピッグの運送費がいくらだと考えていますか。
2. 社長はゴードン教授に何を確認しようとしていますか。

The head of the Tariff Department laughed when he read Flannery's letter. He read it again and became serious.

"Oh, no!" he said. "Flannery is right. Pigs are pigs. ① I'll have to check officially on this." He spoke to the president of the company. ② The president treated the matter lightly. "What is the rate on pigs and on pets?" he asked.

"Pigs thirty cents, pets twenty-five," the head of the Tariff Department answered. "Then of course guinea pigs are pigs," the president said.

"Yes," the head of the Tariff Department agreed. "I look at it that way, too. ③ A thing that can come under two rates is naturally to be charged at the higher one. ④ But are guinea pigs, pigs? Aren't they rabbits?"

"Come to think of it," the president said, "I believe they're more like rabbits. Sort of halfway between pig and rabbit. ⑤ I think the question is this — are guinea pigs of the domestic pig family? I'll ask Professor Gordon. ⑥ He's an expert about such things."

ⒶⒷⒸ 単語・語句の研究

☐ **lightly** [láitli]	副 軽々しく
☐ look at it that way	そのように思う
☐ be naturally to be charged	当然料金を課されるべきである
☐ come to think of it	考えてみると
☐ sort of ～	～のような 例 She is sort of a writer. （彼女は作家のようなものだ）
☐ **halfway** [hæ̀fwéi]	形 中間の
☐ **Gordon** [ɡɔ́ːrdn]	名 ゴードン（(姓)）

解説

① **I'll have to check officially on this.**
- 料金係長のセリフ。
- on は「〜について」の意味。
- this はギニーピッグがブタかどうかということ。

② **The president treated the matter lightly.**
- treat は「〜を扱う、考える」、matter は「問題」の意味。

③ **A thing that can come under two rates is naturally to be charged at the higher one.**
- ③と④は料金係長のセリフ。
- A thing that can come under two rates がこの文の主語。that は関係代名詞で、that can come under two rates が先行詞 A thing を後ろから修飾している。can は「〜でありうる」、come under 〜は「〜の項目に入る、〜に分類される」の意味。
- 〈be 動詞 + to + 動詞の原形〉は「〜することになっている」の意味。ここでは to のあとに be charged と受け身の形が続いている。
- one は rate の言いかえ。

④ **But are guinea pigs, pigs?**
- guinea pigs are pigs を疑問文にしたものだが、pigs が連続してしまうので間にカンマが置かれている。

⑤ **I think the question is this — are guinea pigs of the domestic pig family?**
- ⑤と⑥は社長のセリフ。
- think のあとに接続詞の that が省略されている。
- this と are guinea pigs of the domestic pig family? は同格の関係。
- domestic pig は「家畜用のブタ」、family は「(分類学上の) 科」の意味。

⑥ **He's an expert about such things.**
- expert は「専門家」の意味。

UNIT 3

 **読解のポイント**

1. 32匹だったギニーピッグは、数か月後に何匹まで増えましたか。
2. ゴードン教授の手紙には、何と書かれていましたか。

The president wrote to Professor Gordon. ① Unfortunately, the professor was in South America collecting zoological samples. ② His wife forwarded the letter to him.

The professor was in the Andes. ③ The letter took many months to reach him. In time, the president forgot the guinea pigs. ④ The head of the Tariff Department forgot them. Mr. Morehouse forgot them. ⑤ But Agent Flannery did not. ⑥ The guinea pigs had increased to thirty-two. ⑦ He asked the head of the Tariff Department what he should do with them.

⑧ "Don't sell the pigs," Agent Flannery was told. "They are not your property. ⑨ Take care of them until the case is settled."

⑩ The guinea pigs needed more room. Flannery made a large and airy room for them in the back of his office.

⑪ Some months later he discovered he now had one hundred and sixty of them. ⑫ He was going out of his mind.

⑬ Not long after this, the president of the express company heard from Professor Gordon. It was a long and scholarly letter. ⑭ It pointed out that the guinea pig was not related to the common pig.

🅰🅱🅲 単語・語句の研究

☐ zoological [zòuəládʒikl]	形 動物学の、動物に関する
☐ forward ～	動 ～を転送する
☐ Andes [ǽndiːz]	名 アンデス山脈((南米の大山脈))
☐ in time	やがて 例 In time, the issue will be resolved. (やがてその問題は解決されるだろう)
☐ **property** [prápərti]	名 財産
☐ airy [éəri]	形 風通しのよい、広々とした
☐ go out of one's mind	気が狂う　例 They went out of their minds with anger. (彼らは怒りで正気を失った)

☐ hear from ～	～から便りをもらう
	例 Have you heard from Sarah?
	(サラから連絡はありましたか)
☐ scholarly [skάlərli]	形 学術的な、学問的な

🗨 解説

① **Unfortunately, the professor was in South America collecting zoological samples.**
- unfortunately は「不運にも、あいにく」、sample は「サンプル、試料」の意味。
- collecting zoological samples は分詞構文で、「～して、そして」の意味。

② **His wife forwarded the letter to him.**
- His と him は①の the professor、つまり Professor Gordon をさす。

③ **The letter took many months to reach him.**
- take ... to ～は「～するのに…（時間）かかる」の意味。

④ **The head of the Tariff Department forgot them.**
- them は前文の the guinea pigs をさす。

⑤ **But Agent Flannery did not.**
- did not のあとに forget them が省略されている。

⑥ **The guinea pigs had increased to thirty-two.**
- 過去完了〈had + 過去分詞〉の文。
- increase to ～は「～まで増える」の意味。

⑦ **He asked the head of the Tariff Department what he should do with them.**
- He はどちらも⑤の Agent Flannery をさす。
- what he should do with them は間接疑問〈what + S + V〉で、「Sは何をVするか」の意味。do with ～は「～を扱う、処理する」の意味。them は⑥の The guinea pigs をさす。

⑧ **"Don't sell the pigs," Agent Flannery was told.**
- the pigs は the guinea pigs のこと。

- Agent Flannery was told は過去の受け身の文。

⑨ **Take care of them until the case is settled.**
  - 料金係長のセリフ。
  - them は⑧の the pigs をさす。
  - take care of ～は「～の世話をする」の意味。
  - the case is settled は受け身の文。settle は「～に決着をつける、～を解決する」の意味。

⑩ **The guinea pigs needed more room.**
  - room は「空間、場所」の意味。

⑪ **Some months later he discovered he now had one hundred and sixty of them.**
  - he はどちらもフラナリー氏をさす。
  - discovered のあとに接続詞の that が省略されている。
  - them は⑩の The guinea pigs をさす。one hundred and sixty of them は「160匹のギニーピッグ」の意味。

⑫ **He was going out of his mind.**
  - 過去進行形の文。ここでは「～しかける、～しそうになる」の意味で進行形が使われている。

⑬ **Not long after this, the president of the express company heard from Professor Gordon.**
  - not long after this は「それから間もなく」の意味。
  - the president of the express company がこの文の主語。the express company は「インターアーバン・エクスプレス・カンパニー」をさす。

⑭ **It pointed out that the guinea pig was not related to the common pig.**
  - It は前文の a long and scholarly letter をさす。
  - that は接続詞で、point out that ～は「～ということを指摘する」の意味。that 節は受け身の文。relate ～ to ... は「…と～を関係づける」の意味。つまり、ギニーピッグはふつうのブタとは関係がないということ。

読解のポイント

1. ギニーピッグ1匹の運送費はいくらになりましたか。
2. フラナリー氏はモアハウス氏にいくら請求することになりましたか。

UNIT 3

① The president then told the head of the Tariff Department that guinea pigs are not pigs and must be charged only twenty-five cents as domestic pets. ② The Tariff Department informed Agent Flannery that he should take the one hundred and sixty guinea pigs to Mr. Morehouse and collect twenty-five cents for each of them.

Agent Flannery wired back. "③ I've got eight hundred now. ④ Shall I collect for eight hundred? ⑤ How about the sixty-four dollars I paid for cabbages to feed them?"

Many letters went back and forth. ⑥ Flannery was pushed into a few feet at the extreme front of the office. ⑦ The guinea pigs had all the rest of the room. ⑧ Time kept moving on as the letters continued to go back and forth.

Flannery now had four thousand and sixty-four guinea pigs. He was beginning to lose control of himself. ⑨ Then, he got a telegram from the company, which said "Error in guinea pig bill. Collect for two guinea pigs — fifty cents."

単語・語句の研究

☐ **wire (d)** [wáiər(d)]	動 電報を打つ
☐ **extreme** [ikstríːm]	形 最も端にある、極端な
☐ **move on**	(時間が) 過ぎる 例 While she was trying to come up with a solution, time kept moving on. (彼女が解決策を考えている間にも、時間は進み続けた)
☐ **lose control of oneself**	自制心を失う 例 He never lost control of himself. (彼は決して自制心を失うことはなかった)
☐ **telegram** [téləgræm]	名 電報

☐ **bill** [bil]　　　　　　　图 請求書

 解説

① **The president then told the head of the Tariff Department that guinea pigs are not pigs and must be charged only twenty-five cents as domestic pets.**
- thatは接続詞。
- must be chargedは助動詞mustのあとに受け身が続いている形。〈must be + 過去分詞〉は「～されなければならない」の意味。

② **The Tariff Department informed Agent Flannery that he should take the one hundred and sixty guinea pigs to Mr. Morehouse and collect twenty-five cents for each of them.**
- thatは接続詞。
- heはAgent Flanneryをさす。
- take ～ to ...は「～を…のところへ持っていく」、collectは「（料金など）を徴収する」の意味。

③ **I've got eight hundred now.**
- ③～⑤はフラナリー氏が料金係長に送った電報の内容。
- 現在完了〈have + 過去分詞〉の文。

④ **Shall I collect for eight hundred?**
- Shall I ～?は「～しましょうか」と相手の意志をたずねる表現。

⑤ **How about the sixty-four dollars I paid for cabbages to feed them?**
- How about ～?は「～はどうですか」と相手の意見をたずねる表現。
- I paid for cabbages to feed themがthe sixty-four dollarsを後ろから修飾している。to feed themは「～するための」という意味の不定詞の形容詞的用法で、cabbagesを後ろから修飾している。

  ✐ 確認 （　　）内に適切な語を入れなさい。
  ア．彼は昼食に食べるためのサンドイッチを作った。
  　　He made sandwiches (　　　) (　　　　) for lunch.

イ．その男性は、孫にあげるためのTシャツを買った。

The man bought a T-shirt (　　　) (　　　) to his grandchild.

- cabbageは「キャベツ」、feedは「～にエサを与える」の意味。
- themはギニーピッグをさす。

⑥ **Flannery was pushed into a few feet at the extreme front of the office.**

- 過去の受け身の文。
- push ～ into ...は「～を…に押し込む」、feetは「フィート（長さの単位）」、extremeは「一番端の、先端の」の意味。
- ギニーピッグがオフィスのほとんどを占領しているせいで、フラナリー氏は前の方に追いやられてしまい、最前の数フィートの場所に押し込められたということ。1フィートは30.48センチメートル。

⑦ **The guinea pigs had all the rest of the room.**

- the rest of ～は「～の残り」の意味。

⑧ **Time kept moving on as the letters continued to go back and forth.**

- keep ～ingは「～し続ける」、asは「～する間」、continue to ～は「～し続ける」の意味。

⑨ **Then, he got a telegram from the company, which said "Error in guinea pig bill. Collect for two guinea pigs — fifty cents."**

- whichは関係代名詞（非制限用法）で、「そしてそれは～」とa telegram from the companyについて説明している。
- Error in guinea pig bill.はThere was an error in guinea pig bill.と解釈すればよい。errorは「誤り、間違い」の意味。
- Collect for two guinea pigs — fifty cents.は「ギニーピッグ2匹分、つまり50セントを徴収せよ。」の意味。

読解のポイント

1. フラナリー氏はモアハウス氏に会うことができましたか。
2. フラナリー氏はブタや牛の運送費をいくらにすると言っていますか。

Flannery ran all the way to Mr. Morehouse's home. ① But Mr. Morehouse had moved. ② Flannery searched for him in town but could not find him. ③ He returned to the express office and found that two hundred and six guinea pigs had entered the world since he had left the office.

④ At last, he got an urgent telegram from the main office: "Send the pigs to the main office of the company at Franklin." ⑤ Flannery did so. ⑥ Soon, came another telegram. "⑦ Stop sending pigs. ⑧ Warehouse full." But he kept sending them.

Agent Flannery finally got free of the guinea pigs. ⑨ "Rules may be rules," he said, "but so long as Flannery runs this express office, pigs are pets, and cows are pets, and horses are pets, and lions and tigers and Rocky Mountain goats are pets. ⑩ And the rate on them is twenty-five cents."

⑪ Then he looked around and said cheerfully, "Well, anyhow, it is not as bad as it might have been. ⑫ What if those guinea pigs had been elephants?"

ⒶⒷⒸ 単語・語句の研究

☐ all the way	はるばる 例 They came all the way from Canada. （彼らははるばるカナダからやって来た）
☐ enter the world	生まれる 例 Five puppies entered the world. （5匹の子犬が生まれた）
☐ **urgent** [ə́ːrdʒənt]	形 緊急の
☐ main office	本社
☐ get free of ～	～から解放される　例 I got free of sleep loss.（私は睡眠不足から解放された）
☐ so long as ～ ≒ as long as ～	～する限りは　例 So long as you are our leader, I will do my best.（あなたがリーダーである限りは、私はがんばります）

☐	Rocky Mountain [ràki máuntən]	ロッキー山脈
☐	Rocky Mountain goat	シロイワヤギ((ロッキー山脈産の野生のヤギ))
☐	cheerfully [tʃíərfəli]	圖 機嫌よく
☐	**anyhow** [énihàu]	圖 いずれにしても、とにかく
☐	it is not as bad as it might have been	不幸中の幸いである

 解説

① **But Mr. Morehouse had moved.**
- 過去完了〈had + 過去分詞〉の文。
- move は「引っ越す」の意味。

② **Flannery searched for him in town but could not find him.**
- search for 〜は「〜を探す」の意味。
- him はどちらも①の Mr. Morehouse をさす。

③ **He returned to the express office and found that two hundred and six guinea pigs had entered the world since he had left the office.**
- he はどちらも②の Flannery をさす。
- the express office はインターアーバン・エクスプレス・カンパニーのオフィスのこと。
- that は接続詞。two hundred and six guinea pigs had entered the world も he had left the office も過去完了〈had + 過去分詞〉の文。

④ **At last, he got an urgent telegram from the main office: "Send the pigs to the main office of the company at Franklin."**
- :(コロン)以降が電報に書かれていた内容。
- the pigs はギニーピッグのこと。

⑤ **Flannery did so.**
- so は「そのように」の意味。④の電報の指示に従ったということ。

UNIT 3

⑥ **Soon, came another telegram.**
- 倒置の文。ふつうの語順にすると Soon, another telegram came. となる。

⑦ **Stop sending pigs.**
- ⑦と⑧は電報の内容。
- pigs は the pigs (= the guinea pigs) のこと。文字数を減らすために冠詞の the が省略されている。

⑧ **Warehouse full.**
- ふつうは The warehouse is full. という文だが、冠詞の the と be 動詞が省略されている。
- warehouse は「倉庫」の意味。

⑨ **"Rules may be rules," he said, "but so long as Flannery runs this express office, pigs are pets, and cows are pets, and horses are pets, and lions and tigers and Rocky Mountain goats are pets.**
- run は「～を管理する」の意味。

⑩ **And the rate on them is twenty-five cents.**
- them は⑨の pigs、cows、horses、lions、tigers、Rocky Mountain goats をさす。

⑪ **Then he looked around and said cheerfully, "Well, anyhow, it is not as bad as it might have been.**
- look around は「周りを見回す」の意味。

⑫ **What if those guinea pigs had been elephants?**
- what if ～? は「もし～だったらどうなるか」の意味。
- those guinea pigs had been elephants は仮定法過去完了〈had + 過去分詞〉の文。

  《確認》 (　　) 内に適切な語を入れなさい。
  ア. もしあのときあなたが助けてくれなかったらどうなっていただろう。
  　　What (　　) you had not (　　) me then?
  イ. もし恐竜が絶滅していなかったらどうなっていただろう。
  　　(　　) (　　) the dinosaurs had not become extinct?

確認問題

1 下線部の発音が同じものには○、違うものには×を（　　）に書き入れなさい。

(1) telegram — beneath 　　　（　　　　）

(2) counter — anyhow 　　　（　　　　）

(3) threw — rulebook 　　　（　　　　）

(4) unpleasant — agent 　　　（　　　　）

(5) overcharge — scholarly 　　　（　　　　）

2 ▭ から最も適切な語を選び、（　　）に書き入れなさい。

(1) We had an (　　　　) meeting this morning.

(2) They divided their (　　　　) among their children.

(3) He put his rabbit in a (　　　　).

(4) This issue should not be taken (　　　　).

(5) She left the room and (　　　　) the door.

urgent	slammed	cage	property	lightly

3 日本語に合うように、（　　）内に適切な語を入れなさい。

(1) 彼女はこぶしで机を叩いた。

She hit the desk with her (　　　　).

(2) 名古屋は東京と大阪の中間地点にある。

Nagoya is (　　　　) between Tokyo and Osaka.

(3) 先月の電気代の請求書はどこですか。

Where is last month's electricity (　　　　)?

(4) 睡眠不足は健康に害を及ぼす。

Lack of sleep (　　　　) your health.

(5) もしスケジュールの変更があればお知らせします。

If there are any schedule changes, we will (　　　　) you.

4 日本語に合うように、(　　)内に適切な語を入れなさい。

(1) まだエレンから便りがない。

I haven't (　　　) (　　　) Ellen yet.

(2) 黄色い花であればどんなものでもよい。

Any flower will do, so (　　　) (　　　) it is yellow.

(3) 私はその買い物をクレジットカードで支払った。

I (　　　) (　　　) the purchase with my credit card.

(4) このリストは更新されている。

This list is (　　　) (　　　) date.

(5) 疑問がある場合は、私に質問してください。

If you are (　　　) (　　　), please ask me.

5 次の英語を日本語に訳しなさい。

(1) He bought a pen to use at school.

_____

(2) I want to know what you are worried about.

_____

(3) She ran to me, calling my name.

_____

6 日本語に合うように、[　　]内の語を並べかえなさい。

(1) あなたは彼らが笑っていた理由を知っていますか。

Do you [they / know / laughing / why / were]?

Do you _____?

(2) 彼女は昨日まで1か月間入院していた。

[been / hospital / she / in / had / the] for a month until yesterday.

_____ for a month until yesterday.

(3) もしあのとき道に迷っていたらどうなっていただろう。

[had / I / if / got / what] lost then?

_____ lost then?

7 次の英文を読み、設問に答えなさい。

①Flannery （　　　）（　　　） the book. He ran his hand through the pages and stopped at page sixty-four.

"I won't accept fifty cents," he whispered in an unpleasant voice. "Here's the rule for it: '②When the agent is in any doubt about which of two rates should be charged on a shipment, he shall charge the larger. The person receiving the shipment may put in a claim for the overcharge.' In this case, Mr. Morehouse, I am in doubt. Those animals may be pets. And they may be domestic, but I'm sure they are pigs. And the rulebook says clearly, 'Pigs, Franklin to Westcote, thirty cents each.'"

Mr. Morehouse shook his head bluntly. "Nonsense!" he shouted. "Complete nonsense, I tell you! That rule means common pigs, not guinea pigs!"

"Pigs are pigs," Flannery said firmly.

Mr. Morehouse bit his lip and then ③(fling) his arms out wildly. "Very well!" he shouted. "You shall hear of this! Your president shall hear of this! It is an outrage! I have offered you fifty cents. You refuse it. Keep the pigs until you are ready to take the fifty cents. But, if one hair of those pigs' heads is harmed, I will have the law on you!" He turned and walked out, ④(slam) the door. Flannery carefully lifted the box from the counter and put it in a corner.

(1) 下線部①が「フラナリー氏は、本に手をのばした。」という意味になるように、空所に当てはまる2語の英語を書きなさい。

_____ _____

(2) 下線部②を日本語に訳しなさい。

_____

(3) ③の単語を適切な形に直しなさい。　　　　　_____

(4) ④の単語を適切な形に直しなさい。　　　　　_____

(5) 本文の内容に合うように、次の質問に英語で答えなさい。

How much did Mr. Morehouse want to pay for the two guinea pigs?

_____

8 次の英文を読み、設問に答えなさい。

The president wrote to Professor Gordon. Unfortunately, the professor was in South America collecting zoological samples. His wife forwarded the letter to him.

The professor was in the Andes. The letter took many months to ①(   ) him. In time, the president forgot the guinea pigs. The head of the Tariff Department forgot them. Mr. Morehouse forgot them. But Agent Flannery did not. The guinea pigs had increased to thirty-two. ②He asked the head of the Tariff Department [should / them / what / do / with / he].

"Don't sell the pigs," Agent Flannery was told. "They are not your property. Take care of them until the case is settled."

The guinea pigs needed more room. Flannery made a large and airy room for them in the back of his office. Some months later he discovered he now had one hundred and sixty of them. ③He was going out (   ) (   ) (   ).

Not long after this, the president of the express company heard from Professor Gordon. It was a long and scholarly letter. It pointed out that the guinea pig was not related to the common pig.

(1) 空所①に入る最も適切な語を選び、記号で答えなさい。

　　ア．read　　イ．send　　ウ．reach　　エ．write　　　　　（　　　）

(2) 下線部②が「彼は、それらをどうすべきか料金係長にたずねた。」という意味になるように、[ ]内の語を並べかえなさい。

He asked the head of the Tariff Department _____

_____ .

(3) 下線部③が「彼は気が狂いそうだった。」という意味になるように、空所に当てはまる３語の英語を書きなさい。

_____　_____　_____

(4) 本文の内容に合うように、次の質問に英語で答えなさい。

How many guinea pigs did Mr. Flannery have some months after he made a large and airy room for them?

_____

マイウェイ E.C. Ⅲ

教科書ガイド

解答

READING SKILL 1～8

確認

1　① ア．may be　　　　　イ．may, swimming
　　⑩ ア．how　　　　　　イ．how
5　⑧ ア．written by　　　イ．made by
　　⑨ ア．which surprised　イ．which helped
8　③ ア．singer who　　　イ．who want
　　⑤ ア．where there　　イ．where, rules

LESSON 1

確認

p.34〜36　① ア．named　　　イ．called
　　　　　② ア．Having　　　イ．Being
　　　　　③ ア．how much　　イ．how many
p.37〜40　④ ア．Seen　　　　イ．Written
　　　　　⑩ ア．what I　　　イ．what he

確認問題

1　(1) ×　　(2) ○　　(3) ○　　(4) ×　　(5) ○

2　(1) adopted（彼らのチームは新しい取り組みを採用した）
　　(2) financial（私の祖父母は私に経済的な支援をしてくれた）
　　(3) calling（彼女は海洋生物を保護することが自分の天職だと気づいた）
　　(4) dignify（そのセレモニーに花を添えるため、有名なゲストたちが招待された）
　　(5) supplier（私たちはこの国で最も大きなスマートフォン販売業者だ）

3　(1) biological　　(2) organic　　(3) goodwill　　(4) occupied　　(5) priceless

4　(1) in mind　　(2) devoted herself　　(3) differ from　　(4) compensate for
　　(5) used to

5　(1) そのニュースに驚いて、彼らは静かになった。
　　(2) 宿題がたくさんあるので、私は今夜テレビを見ないだろう。
　　(3) パーティーに来られる人の数を数えましょう。

6　(1) have a daughter named Lily
　　(2) necessary for those who live
　　(3) know how much he got

7　(1) adopting
　　(2) ② エ　　④ ウ
　　(3) the other hand
　　(4) この提案は家に洗濯機のない人々を助けている。
　　(5) (They need to work) For two hours.

8　(1) イ
　　(2) grown
　　(3) 彼女は、地元の農家や業者によって寄付された新鮮な野菜もよく使用する。
　　(4) occupied
　　(5) how much money they have
　　(6) (It has) About 50 seats.

確認

p.45〜47　　⑤ ア．where I　　イ．where he
　　　　　　⑨ ア．have been　　イ．has been
p.48〜51　　② ア．is, that　　イ．was, that[who]
　　　　　　③ ア．were able　　イ．was able

確認問題

1　(1) ○　　(2) ×　　(3) ○　　(4) ×　　(5) ○
2　(1) collision（その車は衝突で損傷を受けた）
　　(2) direct（台風の直接的な影響はないだろう）
　　(3) fundamental（私たちは来週、基本的な英文法を学習します）
　　(4) periodic（彼らは惑星の周期的な運動を観察してきた）
　　(5) trillion（私たちの会社の売り上げは3兆円を超えるだろう）
3　(1) evidence　　(2) practical　　(3) artificially　　(4) Therefore　　(5) target
4　(1) named, after　　(2) thanked, for　　(3) considered to　　(4) proud of
　　(5) able to
5　(1) 私のプリンを食べたのは姉［妹］だった。
　　(2) 私はトマトをいくつか買うためにスーパーマーケットに行った。
　　(3) これは文化祭で撮られた写真だ。
6　(1) the gym where we played
　　(2) have been waiting for our friend
　　(3) They named their dog Mugi
7　(1) ア
　　(2) named after
　　(3) 元素とは、世界にあるものを構成する基本的な物質だ。
　　(4) existing
　　(5) それ以来、科学者たちは新しい元素を人工的につくり出そうとしている。
　　(6) (It was added to the periodic table of elements) In 2017.
8　(1) synthesized
　　(2) ② ウ　　③ イ
　　(3) essential for scientists to conduct
　　(4) 私たちは日本の人々の支援に感謝するために、新しい元素を「ニホニウム」と
　　　名づけた。

確認

p.56〜58	⑨ ア．has worked	イ．has been
p.59〜62	⑦ ア．which is	イ．which was[is]
	⑨ ア．how people	イ．how you
	⑪ ア．helps, grow	イ．help him

確認問題

1 (1) ○　　(2) ×　　(3) ×　　(4) ○　　(5) ○

2 (1) Mint（ミントの葉はフレッシュな香りと味がする）
(2) Morocco（日本はモロッコから大量のタコを輸入している）
(3) chai（チャイを1杯いかがですか）
(4) plantation（この農園ではコーヒーを育てている）
(5) Islam（イスラム教を信仰する人々はムスリムと呼ばれる）

3 (1) popularity　　(2) politics　　(3) crucial　　(4) colonized
(5) Furthermore

4 (1) take root　　(2) case of　　(3) As for　　(4) come up　　(5) it comes

5 (1) 私は赤い自転車を持っているが、それは父が私にくれたものだ。
(2) テーブルを動かすのを手伝ってください。
(3) 私たちは10年間金沢に住んでいる。

6 (1) How people cook rice
(2) This elevator cannot be used
(3) Water consists of hydrogen and oxygen

7 (1) エ
(2) when it comes
(3) イ
(4) 中東の場合、地理は重要な要素である。
(5) They love to drink chai(, strong black tea with sugar).

8 (1) overlooked
(2) ア
(3) believe in
(4) 国によって、お茶の楽しみ方は異なる。
(5) tea helps people relax and
(6) (They frequently drink tea) To satisfy their thirst.

確認

p.67〜69　④　ア．to run　　　イ．time to
　　　　　⑧　ア．to make[cook]　イ．to borrow
p.70〜73　④　ア．make you　　イ．make, room
　　　　　⑪　ア．may, eaten　イ．may be

確認問題

1　(1) ×　　(2) ○　　(3) ×　　(4) ○　　(5) ×
2　(1) unlocked（マイクはついに私たちに心を開いた）
　　(2) location（その地図はレストランの正確な位置を示している）
　　(3) academic（私は彼の学歴を知らない）
　　(4) ability（彼女にはすばらしい芸術の才能がある）
　　(5) accomplish（私たちは目標を達成することができた）
3　(1) clumsy　　(2) potential　　(3) fascinating　　(4) patience
　　(5) training
4　(1) correlate with　　(2) not least　　(3) Even if　　(4) Why don't
　　(5) It, that
5　(1) もし雨なら、その試合は中止されるかもしれない。
　　(2) 彼は彼の兄［弟］を怒らせた。
　　(3) 彼女には今日すべきことがたくさんある。
6　(1) sells a variety of stationery
　　(2) came to Niseko to ski
　　(3) can be used as a
7　(1) folding
　　(2) According to
　　(3) ２次元の物体と３次元の物体を結びつける技能
　　(4) based on
　　(5) １つの折り紙作品を完成させるためには、段階的な指示に従う必要がある。
　　(6) It has four (positive effects).
8　(1) ① your ability to accomplish missions with passion and patience
　　　　③ your skill of performing detailed work with your hands
　　(2) それでも、努力の過程や達成感は必ずあなたによい影響を与えるだろう。
　　(3) Why don't you make origami a habit
　　(4) (They can overcome their clumsiness) By practicing origami repeatedly.

確認

p.78〜81	⑦ ア. reasons why	イ. reason why
	⑫ ア. which	イ. which
p.82〜84	⑨ ア. how	イ. how they

確認問題

1 (1) ○ (2) × (3) × (4) × (5) ×

2 (1) leaners（このクラスは上級学習者用だ）
(2) media（私はソーシャルメディアに写真を何枚か投稿した）
(3) mysteries（私たちは深海の謎を明らかにしたい）
(4) Mass（20世紀初頭に自動車の大量生産が可能になった）
(5) anger（あなたは怒りをコントロールしなければならない）

3 (1) Greek (2) Conversely (3) document (4) pattern
(5) irregular

4 (1) in common (2) instead of (3) read, aloud (4) used to
(5) Thanks for

5 (1) あなたは彼が欠席している理由を知っていますか。
(2) 熊本城は復元中だが、その庭園から見ることができる。
(3) 私は、彼らがそのアイコンをどのようにデザインしたかについての記事を読んだ。

6 (1) to continue to play soccer
(2) her students in the same way
(3) It is fun to learn about

7 (1) 英語のつづりが不規則である主な理由は2つある。
(2) エ
(3) pronounced
(4) ⓐ イ　ⓑ ア
(5) It comes from Italian.

8 (1) the gap between printing technology and language change
(2) ② ウ　③ イ
(3) preserved
(4) Thanks for your help
(5) 英語のつづりや発音が将来どのように変化するのかを予測するのはおもしろい。
(6) Mass printing of documents did.

確認

p.89〜92　④ ア．had, made　　イ．had, been
　　　　　⑥ ア．been, by　　　　イ．have been
p.93〜95　⑨ ア．which, me　　　イ．which, him

確認問題

1　(1) ×　　(2) ×　　(3) ○　　(4) ×

2　(1) examine（彼女はその化石を調べるために、余分な岩石を取り除いた）
　　(2) AI（棋士たちは研究にAIを使用している）
　　(3) Pelicans（ペリカンはすべての鳥類の中で最も長いくちばしを持っている）
　　(4) Anthropologists（人類学者たちは、人類がどのようにアフリカから世界中に移動したのかを研究している）
　　(5) geometric（幾何学模様の着物は初心者におすすめだ）

3　(1) vast　　(2) identified　　(3) civilization　　(4) previous
　　(5) newly

4　(1) in turn　　(2) human-like fingers　　(3) succeeded in　　(4) Nasca Lines
　　(5) vary from

5　(1) 私は、自転車が盗まれたと警察官に言った。
　　(2) 彼はパーティーに来たが、そのことはみんなを喜ばせた。
　　(3) AIは私たちが自動車を運転するのを助ける。

6　(1) have been solved by Emma
　　(2) not only for meat dishes but also
　　(3) at the beginning of April

7　(1) drawn
　　(2) 最も古い絵の一部は、2000年より前につくられた［描かれた］と考えられる。
　　(3) About 1,000 drawings had been found
　　(4) These discoveries have been made by
　　(5) studying
　　(6) He aims to make a map that overviews all the Nasca Lines.

8　(1) the photos of the Nasca Pampa
　　(2) ウ
　　(3) detecting
　　(4) （チームの誰も発見していなかった）人型のような地上絵を、AIが見つけたこと。
　　(5) AI技術を使ってナスカの地上絵を研究することは、AIが幅広い研究分野に貢献しうるということを、私たちに示してくれます。
　　(6) No, he didn't.

確認

p.100〜103　①　ア．has, playing　　イ．has been

p.104〜106　⑥　ア．Having　　　　イ．knowing

確認問題

1　(1) ○　　(2) ○　　(3) ×　　(4) ×　　(5) ○

2　(1) harvest（今年の秋は米が豊作だった）

　　(2) account（銀行口座を開設したいのですが）

　　(3) Despite（一生懸命勉強したにもかかわらず、彼女は試験に落ちた）

　　(4) secretly（彼は彼らの会話をこっそり聞いていた）

　　(5) outbreak（鳥インフルエンザの発生が原因で、卵の価格が上昇した）

3　(1) opposition　　(2) independence　　(3) wisdom　　(4) discard

　　(5) status

4　(1) sold out　　(2) no exception　　(3) out of　　(4) bring about

　　(5) resulted in

5　(1) 私は今することがないので、あなたを手伝える。

　　(2) 私の兄［弟］は、1時間ずっと自分の部屋を掃除している。

　　(3) この道路は昨年まで修理されていなかった。

6　(1) how to pronounce this word

　　(2) so excited that he couldn't sleep

　　(3) must focus on the class

7　(1) ア

　　(2) because[since / as] she was

　　(3) how to recycle

　　(4) had not been established in

　　(5) thrown

　　(6) No, she didn't.

8　(1) エ

　　(2) sold out

　　(3) realizing

　　(4) 女性たちはお金を稼いで自分の銀行口座を開設することができ、そのことは彼
　　　女たちの経済的自立につながった。

　　(5) It banned the use of plastic bags.

確認

p.113〜115	⑤ ア．me to	イ．encouraged to
	⑦ ア．in which	イ．to which
p.116〜118	④ ア．arriving	イ．Getting[Waking] up
	⑤ ア．had, would	イ．were, would
p.119〜121	③ ア．made us	イ．made, help
p.122〜124	② ア．whether[if], should	イ．whether[if], was
	③ ア．whatever you	イ．whatever I

確認問題

1 (1) ○　　(2) ○　　(3) ×　　(4) ○　　(5) ×

2 (1) stiff（私は肩がこっているので、マッサージを受けたい）
(2) required（生徒たちは制服を着なければならない）
(3) disturb（私が仕事をしている間は邪魔をしないでください）
(4) Taiwanese（私たちはさまざまな台湾料理を楽しんだ）
(5) introduction（彼らは新しいシステムの導入を検討している）

3 (1) fell asleep　　(2) opposed to　　(3) around, corner　　(4) make up
(5) In, nutshell

4 (1) エ
(2) 台湾の習慣について聞いて、生徒たちは昼食後に昼寝をするべきだと私は確信しています。
(3) any longer[more]
(4) I understand what you are saying
(5) 特に、私たちはもうすぐ卒業するので、私は友達とおしゃべりをしたいです。
(6) We should take a nap before feeling sleepy.

5 (1) worth a try
(2) 私はたくさん勉強しているのにもかかわらず、それが実を結んでいないとしばしば感じます。
(3) staying
(4) しかし、正直に言って、私は机に頭を横たえた状態で昼寝をしたくありません。
(5) I'm afraid it might have a negative effect
(6) No, she doesn't[does not].

確認

p.128〜130	④ ア．made, excited	イ．him angry
p.131〜133	⑨ ア．can be	イ．be eaten
	⑩ ア．helps, be	イ．be found
p.134〜137	⑤ ア．where	イ．where they
	⑭ ア．had, have	イ．been, passed
p.138〜139	② ア．why she	イ．why, was

確認問題

1 (1) ○　　(2) ×　　(3) ×　　(4) ○　　(5) ×

2 (1) insurance（私の母は保険会社で20年間働いている）
(2) mayor（あなたの市の市長はだれですか）
(3) loyal（彼らはいつも上司にとても忠実だ）
(4) responsibility（私は彼がプロジェクトの責任を取るべきだと思う）
(5) rescued（おぼれていた子どもは無事に救助された）

3 (1) disciplined　　(2) neighbors　　(3) annoyed[irritated]
(4) taxation[taxes]　　(5) complaint

4 (1) provided, with　　(2) what, worse　　(3) In general　　(4) did away
(5) to name

5 (1) なぜ彼女は私のメールに返信しないのだろうか。
(2) 彼がもっと背が高かったら、モデルになっていたかもしれない。
(3) 私は韓国で車を運転したが、そこでは車は右側通行だ。

6 (1) from Emma made me happy
(2) Christmas songs can be heard in
(3) Vitamin C helps iron be absorbed

7 (1) エ　　(2) ア
(3) taken
(4) この税があることで、人々は犬を飼うことに慎重になり、そのことが飼い主の
責任感を強くさせる。
(5) They must pay more than 100 euros.

8 (1) reasons why some cities in Japan did away
(2) さらに、闇取引が横行する可能性があり、そこでは犬が違法に売り買いされる。
(3) ウ
(4) もし犬税があったら、その人はそんなに多くの犬を飼うことをためらったかも
しれない。
(5) Daisuke does.

確認

p.144~146	① ア．found[discovered]	イ．published
	⑤ ア．which, born	イ．which was
p.149~152	③ ア．has been	イ．been eaten
	⑪ ア．help improve	イ．helps reduce
p.153~156	⑧ ア．has, working	イ．has been
	⑭ ア．must be	イ．must, eaten

確認問題

1 (1) ○　　(2) ×　　(3) ○　　(4) ×　　(5) ×

2 (1) possibility（今日は雪の可能性がある）
　　(2) invest（私たちは不動産により多くの資金を投資すべきだ）
　　(3) utilize（彼らは発電するために水力を利用する）
　　(4) constructed（安土城は平地に築かれた）
　　(5) immediately（彼はすぐに警察を呼んだ）

3 (1) disadvantages　　(2) achieve[reach/accomplish]　　(3) outer
　　(4) controversial　　(5) satellite

4 (1) huge amount　　(2) pushed forward　　(3) year by　　(4) Hundreds of
　　(5) eager to

5 (1) 私たちは初めからその試合を見ている。
　　(2) 入浴は睡眠の質を高めるのを助ける。
　　(3) 木星は95個の衛星を持っており、太陽系最大の惑星である。

6 (1) new song has been released
　　(2) knowledge must be shared with
　　(3) flowers painted by the students

7 (1) それには、衛星やロケットの打ち上げ、宇宙ステーションの建設、惑星や衛星の探査が含まれる。
　　(2) sent
　　(3) 国際宇宙ステーションは2011年に建てられ、現在は地球の上空約400キロメートルを周回している。
　　(4) staying
　　(5) far away from
　　(6) It (successfully) brought back rock samples.

8 (1) 近年、日本では毎年3,000億円以上が宇宙開発に費やされている。
　　(2) solving immediate problems rather than investing
　　(3) イ
　　(4) They are called space debris.

確認

p.161～165	⑱	ア．wish, had	イ．wish, were
p.166～169	⑰	ア．had, could	イ．were, buy
p.173～176	⑧	ア．as if	イ．if, had
p.177～180	③	ア．had, would	イ．would have
p.181～184	②	ア．who lives	イ．who gave

確認問題

1 (1) ○　　(2) ○　　(3) ×　　(4) ×　　(5) ○

2 (1) whistled（彼女はお気に入りの曲を口笛で吹いた）

　　(2) grave（私は先週墓参りをした）

　　(3) lane（女の子がうれしそうに小道をかけ下りていった）

　　(4) forgave（彼は私の遅刻を許してくれた）

　　(5) sight（私の姉は視力がよいので、めがねをかける必要がない）

3 (1) as well　　(2) in silence　　(3) apply for　　(4) such, that

　　(5) held out

4 (1) I'm not going to Redmond University

　　(2) decided

　　(3) and keep you cheered up

　　(4) もしあなたがここにいれば、私はとてもうまくやっていけるだろう

　　(5) Mr. Barry does.

5 (1) もしアンが立ち止まって手を差し出さなかったら、彼は黙って通り過ぎただろう

　　(2) I want you to know that

　　(3) forgiven

　　(4) born to be

　　(5) Yes, he is.

┃確認

p.188~191　② ア．listening　　イ．chatting[talking]
　　　　　　③ ア．been　　　　　イ．had lived
p.195~199　⑧ ア．why we　　　イ．why I
　　　　　　⑭ ア．what, ate[had]　イ．what I
p.205~207　⑤ ア．to eat[have]　イ．to give
p.208~210　⑫ ア．if, helped　　イ．What if

┌──────────┐
│ **確認問題** │
└──────────┘

1　(1) ×　　(2) ○　　(3) ○　　(4) ×　　(5) ×
2　(1) urgent（私たちは今朝、緊急会議を行った）
　　(2) property（彼らは子どもたちに財産を分けた）
　　(3) cage（彼はウサギをかごに入れた）
　　(4) lightly（この問題を軽く考えるべきではない）
　　(5) slammed（彼女は部屋を出て、ドアをばたんと閉めた）
3　(1) fist　　(2) halfway　　(3) bill　　(4) harms　　(5) inform
4　(1) heard from　　(2) long as　　(3) paid for　　(4) up to
　　(5) in doubt
5　(1) 彼は学校で使うためのペンを買った。
　　(2) 私はあなたが何を心配しているか知りたい。
　　(3) 彼女は私の名前を呼びながら走ってきた。
6　(1) know why they were laughing
　　(2) She had been in the hospital
　　(3) What if I had got
7　(1) reached for
　　(2) 荷物に２つの料金のどちらが課されるべきかについて係員に疑問があるときは、
　　　　高い方の料金を課すものとする。
　　(3) flung
　　(4) slamming
　　(5) He wanted to pay fifty cents.
8　(1) ウ
　　(2) what he should do with them
　　(3) of his mind
　　(4) He had one hundred and sixty (guinea pigs).

Acknowledgments

Reading 1

Adapted from Lucy Maud Montgomery, "Anne of Green Gables"

Reading 2

Based on Ellis Parker Butler, "Pigs is Pigs"

A

三省堂版・マイウェイ　E. C. III